PAULA CLARK

MORRIS

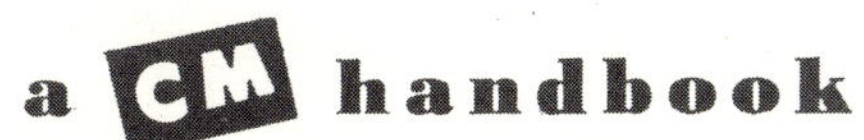

AF412710

THROWING
on the
POTTER'S WHEEL

by THOMAS SELLERS

PROFESSIONAL PUBLICATIONS, INC.
COLUMBUS, OHIO

FOREWORD

FEW THINGS are more intriguing to an observer than watching a skilled potter pull up a pot from a mass of clay spinning on the potter's wheel. This seemingly easy and spontaneous manipulation of clay has lured many of the onlookers into working on the potter's wheel themselves.

Like most techniques, wheel work is deceptive because the potter who makes throwing look easy enough for anyone to do probably has devoted several years to the practice of his craft. Among beginners there are those who find that they have an almost innate sensitivity to clay and the wheel which permits them to make a perfect pot at the first attempt; others have no initial success and must face a long struggle in developing this response to material and tool. There is, however, a fascination about working on the wheel that encourages most beginners to continue.

Undoubtedly the best method of learning to use the wheel is to watch a practicing potter and work with him. Direct contact with a teacher certainly will enable one to learn more quickly and efficiently since the student can observe, question and be corrected at will. Unfortunately, many of those who would like to try wheel work have no such guide available to them. It is mainly to these would-be student potters that this book is dedicated. Lacking the opportunity to work with, or even to observe a good potter, the beginner should be able to learn the fundamentals of working on the potter's wheel by following the text and illustrative photographs of the various processes. No doubt, this method probably will take longer than a more direct one because the "teacher" cannot point out mistakes and make corrections, but with study and persistent practice, the techniques can be learned.

Let me emphasize that there is no *one* or *correct* method of throwing. Each potter develops his own way of working, which is influenced by his physical make-up, materials, wheel construction, and perhaps a combination of any or all of these. There are nearly as many methods of working as there are potters. The beginner must realize that *any* method from which he starts may be modified later to suit his particular needs.

Certain steps in the throwing process, however, are basic: the beginner must follow these in order to have any success whatever on the wheel. We are primarily concerned here with these basic steps or processes — from the wedging of the clay to the making of specific shapes.

In addition to the photographs demonstrating the various problems involved in beginning throwing, many illustrations of wheel-thrown pottery are included which represent the work of contemporary American potters. These were selected to illustrate the various treatments of shapes with which the chapters are concerned and to show some of today's trends in pottery-making in America.

Thomas Sellers
1960

CONTENTS

All Rights Reserved
*This book, or parts thereof, may not be reproduced in
any form without written permission of the publishers.*

First Edition December 1960

Second Printing February 1963

Third Printing November 1964

Fourth Printing September 1968

ACKNOWLEDGMENTS

The author wishes to express his appreciation to Louis G. Farber for the many photographs illustrating the step-by-step processes, and Joseph Schmidt for the layout and design.

Library of Congress Catalog Card Number: 61-22363

Copyright 1960

PROFESSIONAL PUBLICATIONS, INC.
COLUMBUS, OHIO

Publishers of *Ceramics Monthly* Magazine

Printed in U.S.A.

1

TOOLS AND CLAY

DEVELOPMENT OF THE WHEEL

1. Indian Potter Maria Martinez shapes a bowl on a primitive forerunner of the potter's wheel. The coil-built pot is started inside the bottom of a shell-like form which is easily turned on a flat surface.

Photo credit: New Mexico State Tourist Bureau

ONE OF THE most abundant materials on the earth is clay. Primitive peoples found that this extremely plastic and responsive material, which dried hard in the sun, could be used for making containers for storing their food as well as for making bricks for their buildings.

The making of pottery almost certainly originated in connection with the making of baskets. It is assumed that primitive man used clay to line woven reed baskets to make them more practical for storing grain and other dry food, and that through this use of clay he discovered that it could be baked and made harder than by sun drying. This important discovery may have come about when a clay-lined basket accidentally fell into a fire, with the result that the advantages of exposing clay to intense heat became apparent.

It is possible that baskets continued to serve as forms for the clay liners and were burnt off in the fire that hardened the clay. Eventually the potter decided that he could do without the basket mold or form, and modeled his pottery "freehand." These early pots, formed from coils or slabs of clay, were shaped and decorated in imitation of the baskets which inspired them.

The early potter affixed his clay to a stationary stand around which he walked, shaping his pot as it grew under his hands. Later, potters facilitated their hand-building methods by starting their pottery inside shell-like forms — the bottom of a gourd or the bottom piece of a broken pot — which could be rotated easily and rapidly on a flat stone (Figure 1). Thus, the pot was provided with a shaped bottom for its beginning and the potter was relieved of the necessity of walking around the pot while working.

Eventually, this device was improved upon even further. A horizontal disc-like surface, which was pivoted on a post sunk in the ground, was substituted for the mold-like base. The clay was placed on this stand which the potter revolved with one hand while he formed the clay into a circular-shaped pot with the other hand. Naturally, this process had obvious drawbacks, but subsequent developments in the potter's wheel freed both the potter's hands for direct manipulation of the clay.

Very early wheels were probably much like the primitive wheels still in use today in some of the Asiatic countries. A collar on the underside of the wheel centers it on a shaft stuck in the ground, the weight of the wheel keeping it in place. The stone or wooden wheel is turned either by direct rotation with the hands or by means of a removable stick placed in one of several notches or holes near the outside of the top of the wheel. The spinning wheel gains enough momentum for the potter, squatting on the ground over his work, to complete a pot before the wheel comes to a standstill (Figure 2).

A later development of the potter's wheel, one which still is in general use today, consists of a lightweight wheel head connected by a shaft to a heavy balance wheel which revolves in a socket set in its base. This type of wheel, known as a direct-kick wheel, is rotated by means of kicking directly upon the top surface of the balance wheel from a sitting position, while the hand work is done on the wheel head above (Figure 3).

The treadle wheel, a later development, has a balance wheel and wheel head connected by a shaft, like the direct-kick type. But in addition, it has a crank and treadle arrangement connected to the balance wheel. This wheel is operated by kicking the treadle instead of the balance wheel, and it can be operated either from a standing or sitting position, according to the design of the wheel. Like its forerunner, the direct-kick wheel, the treadle wheel is in general use today.

Many other changes and refinements have been made on the potter's wheel during the thousands of years of its existence. In the 17th Century, a pulley arrangement was devised whereby an assistant turned a connecting wheel to supply power. A 19th Century innovation was a steam-driven wheel. Our own 20th Century contribution has been the electric wheel, and the best of these give good speed control and nearly vibration-free performance.

In the pottery world today, work is performed on all types of wheels. Indian potters work on the primitive forefunner of the wheel — the revolving potsherd. Oriental potters still use the same type of wheel their forefathers used, while many potters in the western world work on the variable-speed motorized wheel, the latest advancement in wheel development. The modern potter has many models and types from which to choose. If the wheel he is working on seems to others to be a primitive model, its use probably is due not to necessity but because that wheel does what he wants it to do better than a newer model.

2. Primitive wheel still in use in India is balanced on a shaft sunk in the ground and rotated by use of a removable stick. Momentum of the turning wheel frees both of the potter's hands for shaping the clay.

3. Kick wheel, operated by the potter from a seated position, is turned by kicking the large balance wheel. A shaft connects the balance wheel to the turntable above, on which the pottery is made.

Photo credit: Ann Moore

SELECTION OF A WHEEL

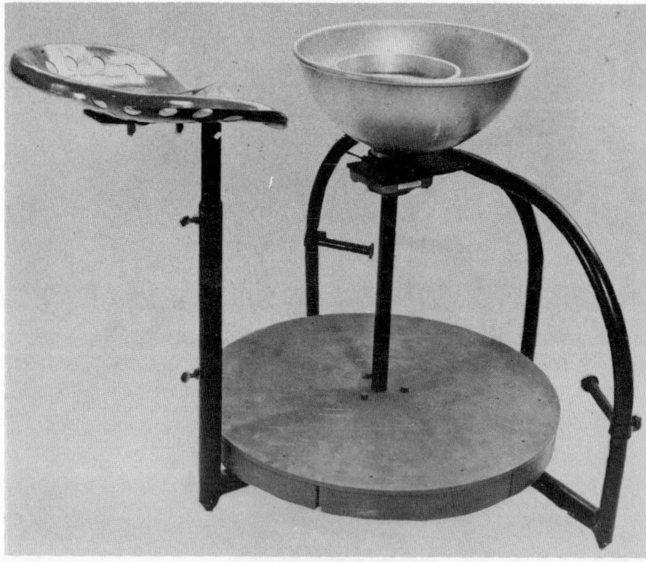

Direct kick wheel, operated from a sitting position by kicking the heavy balance wheel, is the modern equivalent of the traditional kick wheel. Because of the weight of the balance wheel, constant kicking is not necessary.

—Randall wheel

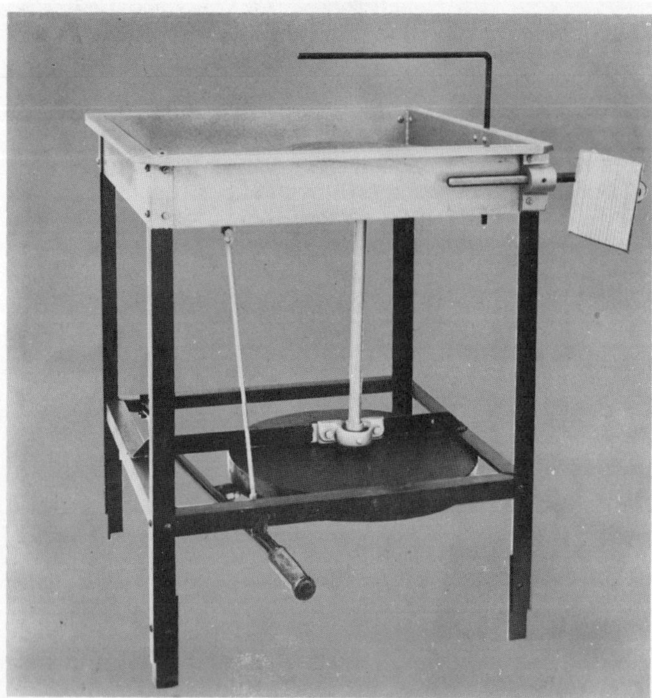

Treadle kick wheel has a crank and treadle arrangement connected to the balance wheel. Operated from a standing position, this wheel is rotated by kicking the treadle instead of the balance wheel itself.

—Klopfenstein wheel

IN SELECTING a wheel for his use, the potter's final choice should be made on the basis of price, available space for the wheel, style preference, and possibly his physical requirements or limitations.

The choice of a wheel may be influenced by price. Naturally, the higher-priced wheels have advantages over the others, but the wheel of any reputable manufacturer is acceptable for beginning work. If the potter wishes to continue later on a better wheel, he can, of course, replace the first with a better one. Inexpensive wheels may cost from $60 to $100, better ones around $150, while the best power wheels may be priced as high as $350.

Because wheels vary in size, the space available for placing the wheel in the home, studio or garage might influence the selection of wheel type. If the space available is limited, perhaps a small wheel will be the only solution. A prospective wheel purchaser must consider that some of the larger wheels cannot be passed through standard doorways or cannot be moved up and down stairways.

Selection of a wheel type or style might also be influenced by the geographic location of the potter. The potter's choice might be determined by the type of wheel in popular use in the area where he lives. Craftsmen of certain areas of the country seem to have decided preferences for certain wheel styles — perhaps a power wheel over a treadle-kick wheel. And if a student learns to throw on another's wheel, the chances are that he will wish to continue using that type when he purchases his own wheel.

Physical limitations or disabilities of the potter are important considerations when selecting a wheel. Leg or back difficulties might make the use of a kick wheel inadvisable or impossible, and the choice would have to be made from the various electric wheels on the market.

The problem of selecting a wheel can best be solved by talking with other potters, reading available literature about wheels, and trying out the various types.

Kick wheels depend on foot power for their motion. Although the kicking process may seem

—B & I Electric Wheel

strange and awkward for a beginner, it very quickly becomes virtually automatic. Coordination is soon developed between the hands working on the clay and the feet supplying the desired speed and control.

The *direct kick wheel* is one of the oldest types still in general use today. The potter sits on a bench (which is part of the wheel construction) and turns the heavy flywheel by kicking it with his feet; this action in turn revolves the wheel head on which the clay is formed. The momentum gained by the preliminary kicking often is enough to sustain motion throughout the throwing process when a small or medium-sized pot is being made.

The *treadle kick wheel,* a variant of the direct kick wheel, is rotated by kicking a lever or treadle instead of the flywheel. This treadle is attached by a crank arrangement to the shaft and flywheel. Generally, this type has a large pan, or sunken area, around the wheel head which is convenient for holding the water pan, tools, and other equipment needed during throwing. There are several styles of treadle wheels. With one, the potter stands on his right foot and kicks the horizontally-moving treadle with his left; there are also wheels which reverse this stance. Another wheel requires the potter to stand and operate a vertically-moving treadle up and down, much like the motion of a manually-operated sewing machine. At still another wheel the potter sits over his work (as in the direct kick) while kicking the treadle.

In the *electric wheel* a motor replaces foot power. This wheel may be operated from either a standing or sitting position, according to the wheel construction. A power wheel can help to speed up the learning process: since co-ordination between feet and hands is not necessary, the student is free to concentrate on the work his hands are doing. The power wheel also may be considered advantageous to the advanced potter, since its use reduces fatigue and thus speeds up the production of pots. The power wheel might be the only possible choice for some potters, since it generally is smaller and occupies less space and is easier to move. The potter-to-be who is selecting an electric wheel should be certain the wheel has a variable speed control.

Another kick wheel in use today is a treadle type operated from a sitting position. Potters who spend many hours every day on the wheel in production work find the sitting position less tiring.

—Foster wheel

The electric wheel, the latest advance in the evolution of the potter's wheel, relieves the potter of the necessity of kicking for power. Wheel speed is controlled by a foot lever on most electric wheels.

—Skutt wheel

—Craftool Electric Wheel

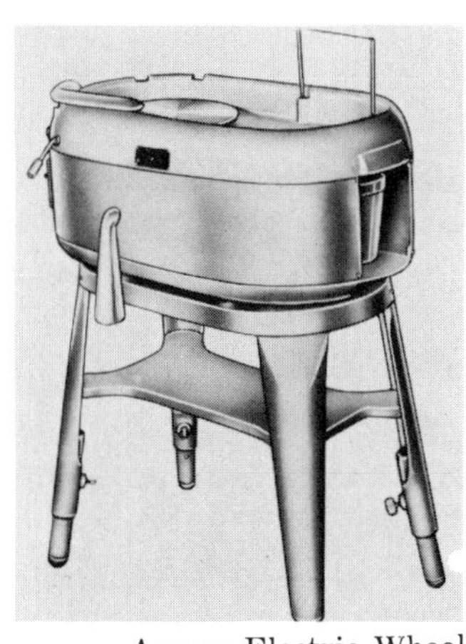

—Amaco Electric Wheel

ACCESSORY TOOLS

THE HANDS in contact with the clay on the wheel are the most important tools used in throwing. But there are other pieces of equipment and tools necessary in the throwing process. None of these is expensive, and many of them can be improvised. Most of your equipment can be kept together in one container — perhaps a fishing tackle box or, eventually, in one of your own finished pots! Tools should be kept clean and ready for use. Metal tools should be wiped dry after each throwing session.

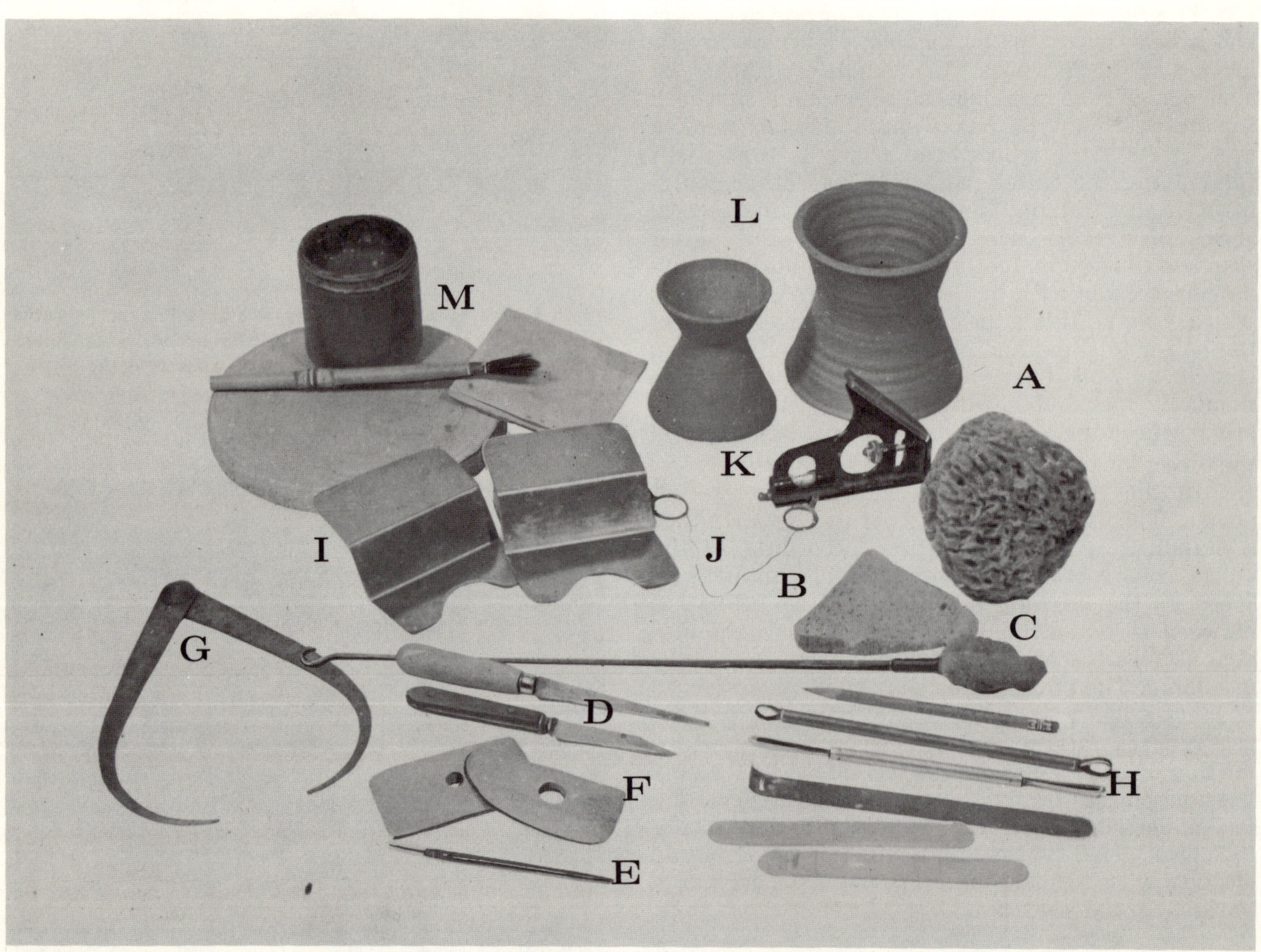

A. Large Natural Sponge, to lubricate hands and clay with water and to clean up the wheel and the potter after work.

B. Elephant Ear Sponge, fine-textured and flat, convenient for finishing work such as removing or subduing throwing marks on pots.

C. Sponge on Stick can be a small silk sponge or retired scrap of large sponge, used to swab water from the inside of tall pots.

D. Potter's Knife or a paring knife, to cut clay from wedged lump and to release pots from bats and tiles.

E. Pointer, to probe and destroy air pockets and to cut uneven or excess clay from rims. Can be made by grinding crochet hook to a sharp point.

F. Wooden Ribs, used inside or outside the pot wall to aid in shaping and drawing up clay wall.

G. Calipers, to obtain exact measurements for duplicating exact sizes, and to make lids fit pots.

H. Foot Rimmers are rigid steel or wire tools used in cutting foot rims on bottoms of pots.

I. Lifters are used to remove pots from wheel head and transfer them to tiles or bats.

J. Cutting Wire is a fine wire attached to end pieces, for cutting pots free of the wheel head.

K. Level is useful in positioning bottle shapes in chucks for foot rimming.

L. Chucks are thrown forms, bisque-fired, in which small-necked pots are inverted to stabilize them for foot rimming.

M. Plaster Bats and Tiles can be attached to the wheel head with slip; pots thrown on these are easy to remove from the wheel. Bats are made of plaster of Paris cast in pie tins.

CHOICE OF A CLAY

JUST AS THE WHEEL is the potter's essential machine, so is clay the essential material needed for throwing. And the choice of a clay to meet the individual potter's requirements is equally important as the selection of a wheel.

Clay is the result of the weathering and decomposition of feldspathic rocks over a very long period of time. Pure clay is unsuitable for direct use in pottery making since it shrinks and warps too much; its main use to the potter is in the compounding of glazes and special clay bodies.

Natural clay, which can be used as it comes from the ground with a minimum of refining or other preparation, contains impurities which lower its firing temperature and impart plasticity, and thus make it desirable for the potter's use.

To be manipulated easily on the wheel, a throwing clay must be quite *plastic* and it must retain its shape while responding to the pressure of the hands.

Some clays are "short"; that is, they lack the necessary degree of plasticity for easy handling. Such clays tend to crack and even break apart while being manipulated. To make such a clay acceptable for use, it can be combined with a very plastic clay.

Plasticity of clay often improves upon aging. Very often a clay that is too "short" develops an adequate degree of workability after it is processed and aged. Plasticity of a clay also may be improved by adding to it a very small percentage of bentonite which must be added to the dry powder form of the clay.

A satisfactory clay must be able to *absorb* considerable quantities of water without losing its shape by slumping or deforming. The beginner on the wheel probably will use an excessive amount of water for lubricating his clay and hands until such time when he has gained more skill in working. The clay he uses during the learning process must be able to withstand this water soaking.

A good throwing clay must also be *porous*. This property allows the water to escape during the drying process so the piece doesn't crack or warp. One way to produce porosity in a clay that lacks this quality is to add grog to the clay. Grog is a fired clay that has been crushed and screened to a specific particle size. The amount of grog added to clay varies with individual potters, but amounts from 10% to 50% generally are used.

Choice of a clay for use in throwing depends on factors other than workability. The principal one is the *maturing temperature* in firing the finished ware. The maturing point of the clay must correspond to the maximum temperature of the kiln's firing range. That is, if the available kiln is made for a maximum firing of 2000°F., you must use a clay that matures at or below that temperature.

Availability is of great importance in selecting a clay for your use. A locally - available clay can save a potter much money in shipping charges. In a number of areas, potters can dig and process their own clay if it is found to be relatively free from pebbles, rocks and excess sand.

When purchasing clay, the *form* in which it arrives may be important. Many potters prefer a clay that comes moist and ready-to-use, saving them the bother of mixing it. Buying clay in a powder form is cheaper, however, since the potter isn't paying for the transportation of water.

CLAY TYPES

Earthenware is the lowest-firing clay; it is often referred to as a common clay, brick clay or sewer-pipe clay. Its firing range is approximately from cones 06 to 1 (1841° to 2057° F.). In color it ranges from a buff to a red-brown. If it is made up from oxides in the studio, it may be white-firing. Its chief advantages are its abundance—making it relatively inexpensive—and its low-maturing temperature—making it cheaper to fire. Earthenware is a rather coarse-grained material and is generally used in relatively heavy wall sections; consequently, it is a good clay for the beginner's use.

Its principal disadvantage is that it cannot be fired to full vitrification (hard enough to prevent water from passing through the walls) without danger of slumping or deforming. Because of this, earthenware isn't as strong as higher fired clays and is chipped and broken easily. The use of glazes strengthens it and makes it waterproof.

Stoneware clays are in the medium-to-high firing range, maturing from cones 6 to 12 (2174° to 2390°F.). Like earthenware, stoneware is relatively inexpensive. However, it is finer grained and usually is thrown in thinner wall section. It is the clay preferred by most studio potters today. Stoneware can be used as dug from the ground, or it can be compounded for special requirements. Stoneware is fired to vitrification. Its color ranges from a light buff or gray to deep brown and red.

Porcelain is the highest-firing of the clays the potter uses. Since it doesn't occur naturally in the earth it must be compounded. Its special advantages are an extreme hardness and strength when fired (about cone 12, or 2390°F.), a translucent quality in thin wall section, and a clear ringing tone when struck. Porcelain isn't very plastic, and consequently is rather difficult to throw. It has a very sophisticated quality and generally is favored only by the advanced potter who has developed enough technical skill to work with this aristocrat of the clays.

PREPARATION OF THE CLAY

BEFORE ANY WORK can be started on the potter's wheel, the moist clay must be made workable by a process called *wedging*. This consists of working the clay in a manner that removes air bubbles or pockets and produces a uniform texture.

Air bubbles in the clay are one of the main causes of annoyance to the potter—especially the beginner. He usually has more than enough to occupy his attention without having to contend with this extra trouble. These air pockets, which feel like little rocks in the clay, can prevent the potter from completing his work accurately.

Wedging is important also in producing uniformity of texture in the clay. Unless the clay is the same consistency throughout, the thrower will have difficulty in coping with the contrasting hard and soft parts of his clay lump. Careful preparation of the clay by wedging can eliminate these hazards; it should never be slighted as being unimportant.

The process by which the potter rids his clay of these troubles is one of cutting the clay lump into two parts, then slamming one part onto the other on the wedging table or board. This process is repeated until the pockets of air are forced from the clay and a consistent texture of the lump results.

The wedging board itself is a sturdy bench or table of a convenient height—slightly lower than waist high—with a diagonally-stretched taut wire at one end. The wire is used to cut the lump into two parts. The table surface may be a heavy slab of plaster or a solid wooden surface covered with cotton drill or canvas.

1. Enough moist clay is taken from the storage bin for several attempts on the potter's wheel. The mass of clay is held in both hands over the cutting wire on the wedging board, then is brought down through it.

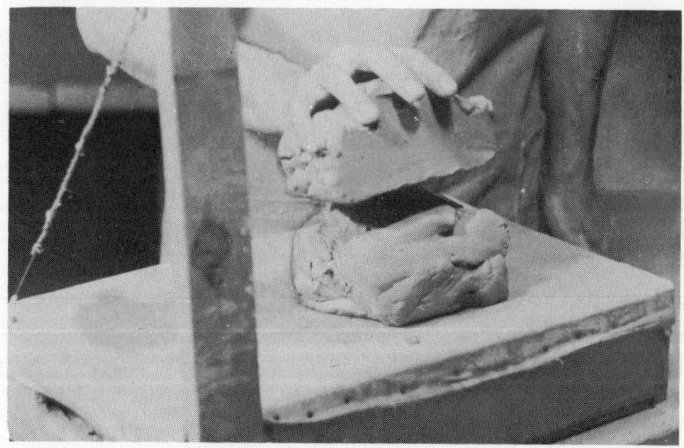

3. The left-hand section is thrown down onto the table, cut-side out. The right-hand part is slammed heavily onto the first, also cut-side out. The right hand stays on its clay until the two sections are joined together.

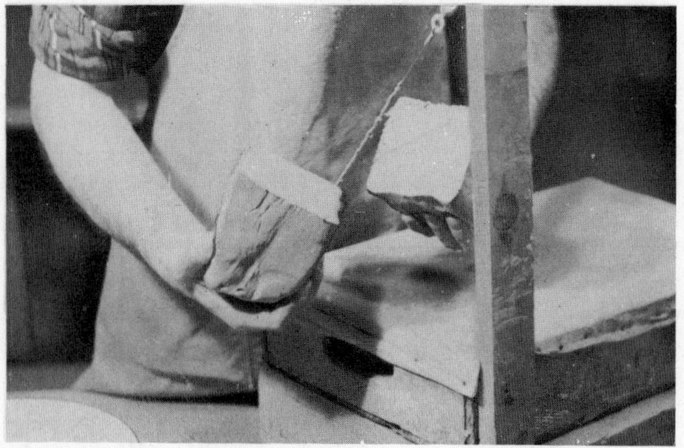

2. Cutting divides the clay lump into two parts. The presence of air bubbles or pockets is noted by glancing at the cut sections of the clay after this action. One purpose of wedging is to rid the clay of these air bubbles.

4. When this sequence has been repeated many times, the potter shapes the clay into a loaf. Holding the two ends of the lump, he pats it down onto the table to form four sides, carefully avoiding working creases into the clay.

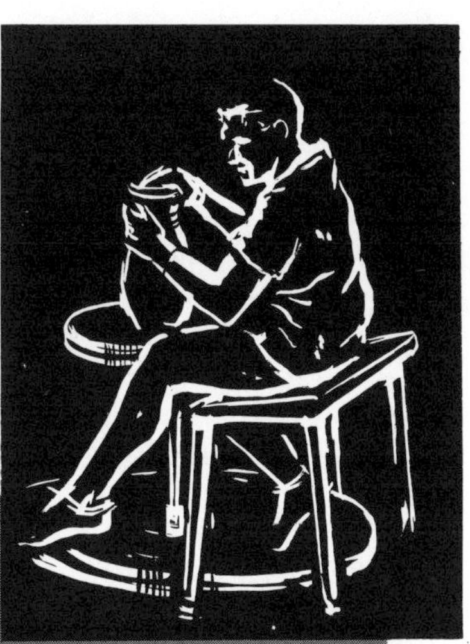

2

FUNDAMENTALS OF THROWING

CENTERING

THROWING, the name applied to working on the potter's wheel, probably got this designation from the potter's first action in making a pot on the wheel. His first step is to *throw* the clay onto the wheel head.

The procedure used to attach the clay to the wheel head may vary according to the type of wheel being used. If it is equipped with a standard metal wheel head, the clay may be thrown directly onto the dry metal table. If the wheel has a plaster head or is the drop-head type on which throwing is done on plaster bats, the surface of the plaster must be dampened with water before starting. Otherwise there is a possibility that the clay will not adhere should the plaster absorb too much moisture from the clay where it meets the bat.

Centering is the first and most important step in learning to work on the potter's wheel. All succeeding steps depend on the accuracy of the centering process, and the principle involved is in constant use throughout the entire processes of throwing. Unless this step is accomplished accurately, the pot will not be symmetrical, and unless symmetry is achieved, there is no point in using the wheel. Mastery of this vital step may not come easily to the beginner, but when centering is accomplished and can be done repeatedly, the rest of the techniques will be more easily acquired.

The speed at which the wheel is rotated is very important for successful throwing. The initial process requires the highest speed, and each succeeding step is accomplished by using a lower speed. Speed usually is indicated by revolutions per minute (rpm), but it is difficult to look at a turning wheel and determine its speed. To designate the speeds required for various steps, a simplified "speed scale" will be used: when the wheel is rotating at near-maximum speed, it will be called a speed of *four;* when it is at a standstill, *zero.* Speed *one* is slow; medium speed, *two,* and medium-fast, *three.*

Before starting to work, the beginner should have his tools and equipment on hand at the wheel.

A large natural sponge and a pan of water are needed for lubricating the clay and hands, and these may be placed in the recessed basin area of the wheel where the throwing water is caught.

A paster bat, on which to place the used wet scrap clay for drying, should be kept up out of the basin area of the wheel so that it doesn't become water soaked.

The beginner also needs a pencil or pointer of some sort to aid in determining when the clay is centered.

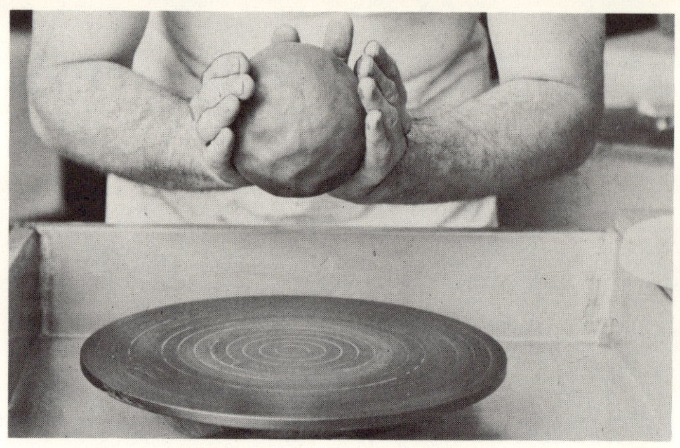

1. A lump of well-wedged clay is patted into a smooth, round ball; a convenient size ball for beginners is shown. The clay is held firmly in both hands and <u>thrown</u> down onto the center of the wheel head with enough force to make it stick securely. The concentric lines inscribed on most wheel heads are guides for correct placement of the clay. The wheel is not yet in motion.

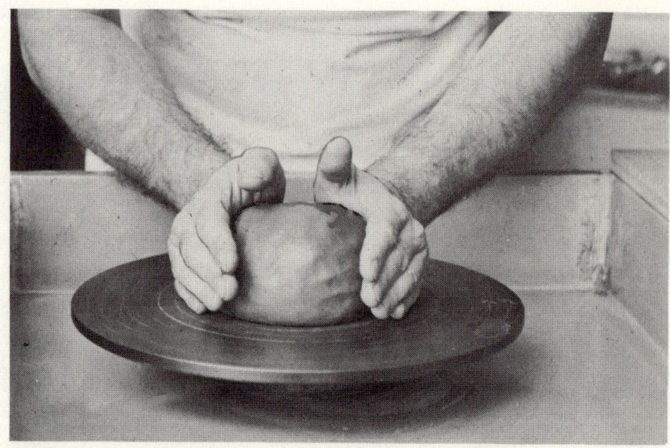

2. The clay lump is patted inward and down, to place it more accurately in the center and to hold it more firmly to the wheel. If a bad aim results in the clay being far off the center, it should be removed and thrown down again. Now the clay must be centered; that is, it must be shaped into a true circular form having the same axis as that of the wheel.

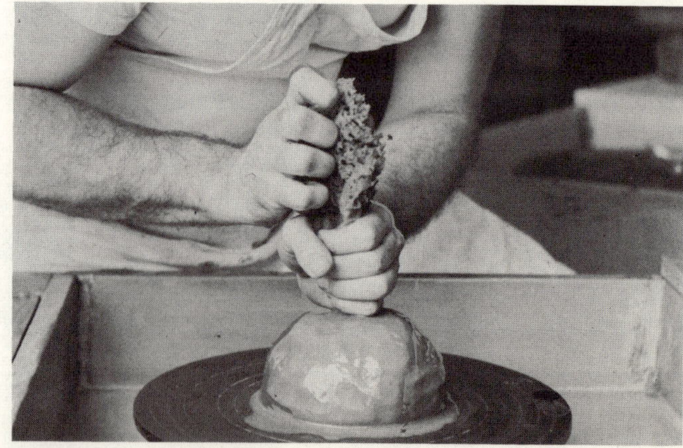

3. Hands and clay are lubricated with water from the sponge, and the wheel is set in motion, <u>counter-clockwise</u>, at <u>speed four</u> (see text for discussion of wheel speeds). Use just enough water to keep the hands from sticking to the clay; too much water tends to weaken the clay. The body should be supported against the frame of the wheel for additional control while working.

4. The hands are brought down and in on the clay. Both arms rest on the wheel frame for extra support and control. Hand pressure is <u>in</u> with the right hand and <u>down</u> with the left. The left hand rides directly across the center of the top of the lump, exerting just enough downward pressure to keep the clay from rising out of the desired shape of a truncated cone.

5. The right hand, pressing in, does most of the work and exerts the greatest control. The fingers are held tightly together at a downward angle to the clay, so that the third and fourth fingertips ride the wheel head for support. Think of the right hand as being a lathe, moving steadily in on the mass of clay to be changed. The left hand supports and strengthens the right.

6. Centering continues with a series of attacks and releases on the clay lump. The fingers of the right hand slowly move in on the clay at the lump base and ride for a short time, still exerting pressure. Then their control is released and the fingers of both hands leave the clay. If pressure is applied and released too abruptly, the work accomplished up to this point will be ruined.

7. Centering is completed by using the right hand in another manner. Knuckle the forefinger and press <u>in</u> at the top half of the lump, then move <u>down</u> the wall to the wheel head. This process gives more control than the three-finger method, but most beginners find it ineffective until their centering is nearly true. The left hand maintains its position while the right hand slides past.

8. Eventually the potter knows by feel alone when his clay is centered, but the beginner usually needs some guide. A clay lump can be tested for centering by supporting a pencil or pointer against the wheel frame and gradually moving it in toward the spinning clay wall until it almost touches. If the space between the clay and the pencil is constant, the clay is centered.

CENTERING

1. The cone method of centering is begun by grasping the clay rigidly between the two hands. Let the clay rise in the center into a tall, pointed shape. As in the other method, wheel speed must be rapid, the clay and hands should be lubricated with water whenever needed, and the body and arms should be supported.

ANOTHER METHOD of centering is illustrated on this page. Any method that helps the beginner center his clay is a *correct* technique for him to use. There is no single method that is better than another, and this is as true in subsequent steps in throwing as it is in centering. It is wise to try every available method and retain any part that makes working easier and quicker. Through experimentation and adaptation, the potter develops his own individual method of controlling the clay. This control is essential in every part of the throwing process and must be developed in this very first step of centering the clay.

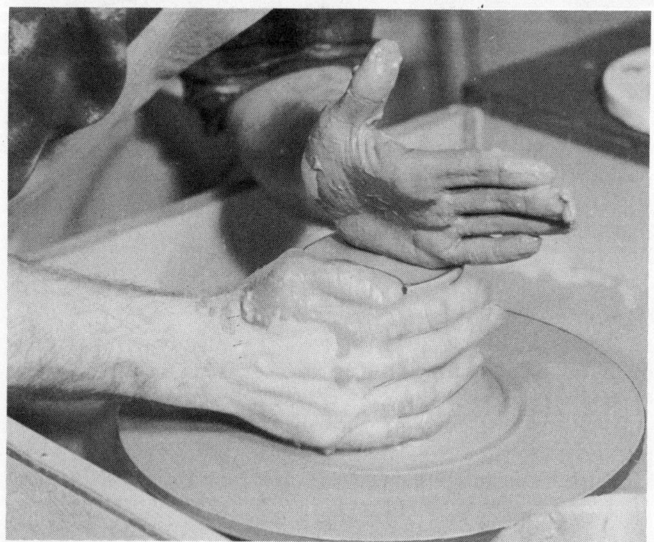

2. After the clay is drawn up into a tall cone shape, it is brought down to a lower level by pressing the top with the left hand. Meanwhile, the side of the clay lump is controlled and kept true by the continued support of the right hand. The hand positions for this step are somewhat similar to those in the first method described.

3. This process — of drawing up and pressing down the cone — is repeated several times. Sometimes the thumbs are used in place of the left hand in lowering the cone. This centering method is good for discovering and breaking air pockets in the clay. Because the hands do not brace one another, more rigid control is necessary.

OPENING

WITH THE CLAY centered on the wheel, the next step is opening the lump to form the inside bottom of the pot. The same discipline necessary for centering is needed for this process: the potter must exercise full control of the clay and keep it centered continually.

Different approaches are used in opening for the two basic pottery shapes, the cylinder and the bowl. The cylinder opening is presented first for two reasons: first, the cylinder is used to make a greater variety of shapes, and second, more skill is required to master this shape. Too frequently, beginners who start with the easier bowl approach find it very difficult, if not impossible, to proceed to cylindrical forms.

3. The inside diameter of the cylinder is established next. The thumbs slowly move away from the center and **toward** the fingers which are riding on the outside of the clay lump. The interlocked thumbs move straight out from the center, resisting the urge to ride up or push down. The resultant bottom must be flat. The thumbs spread the opening until the desired inside diameter is reached.

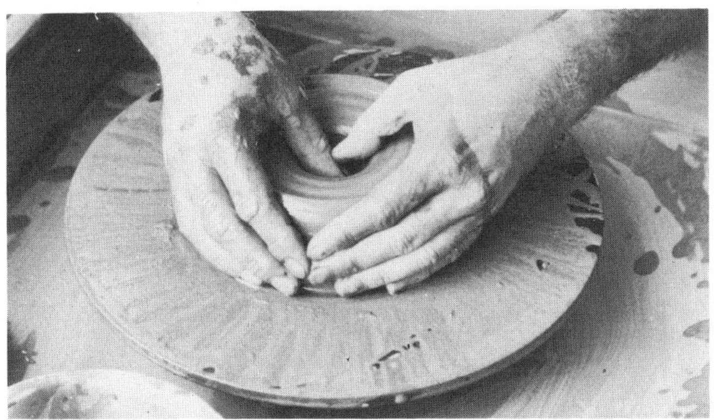

1. The thumbs gradually press **straight down** toward the wheel head, staying firmly in the center of the lump. The need for control is ever-present; note how the forearms are supported on the wheel frame and how the fingertips of the two hands are braced against each other. Lubricate the clay and hands with water whenever necessary. Keep the wheel speed constant at speed three.

4. Now the thumbs move slowly upward, at a right angle to the bottom and straight to the top. If a roll of clay rises to the top during this step, it is pressed down into the top with the fingers. The rim of the wall is grasped by two fingers of the left hand while the right-hand thumb presses the excess clay down; this prevents the roll of clay from peeling off and keeps the rim true.

2. Enough clay is left in the base to provide a bottom wall and thickness for a foot rim. From one-half to three-quarters of an inch should be enough. Amount of thickness can be checked by inserting a broom straw or pin in the center of the opening through the clay to the wheel. If too much thickness remains in the base the opening can be made deeper before proceeding.

5. A cross section of an opened lump shows the basic shape from which the cylinder will rise. The inside opening is not as easy to test for centering as is the outside. The right-hand thumb and middle finger, held like a C-clamp, slowly move in on the spinning clay, freezing into position when they barely touch the clay. Clay is centered if the fingers touch evenly all around the clay, inside and out.

MAKING A CYLINDER

THE LAST BASIC process in making a cylinder shape on the potter's wheel is raising the clay to make the wall. Wheel speed is reduced again, this time to *two*. The right hand does most of the active work in raising the wall. The left hand supports the inside wall by exerting just enough resistance to the right hand pressure to prevent the wall from being pushed to the center. The beginner must remember that the inside diameter of the opening should remain the same as when it was opened and that the wall should be formed *straight up* from this original position. To accomplish this, the potter must learn to keep centered and in constant control of the clay and wheel. The cylinder shape is the basic form from which the potter makes vases, mugs, pitchers, bottles and many other vertical forms. Characteristics of the cylinder are a flat inside bottom opening, vertical walls and a shape usually taller than it is wide.

1. **Raising the wall is begun with the wheel speed reduced to** _two._ **The right hand rides easily but firmly on the wheel head, then gradually presses into the clay lump at the base, using either the tip of the middle finger or the forefinger knuckle, until a roll of clay appears above the pressure. The middle finger of the left hand rides at the inside base, exerting a gentle pressure outward. The two hands are interlocked for added support.**

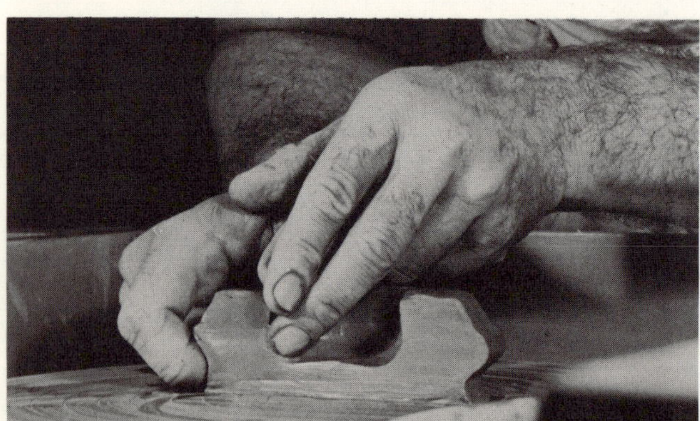

2. **The cross section shows the position of the two hands. The outside knuckle or finger forms the roll of clay to be brought up into a wall. The inside finger, slightly bent for more strength, waits until the outside pressure rises to its level. At that time, the inside finger exerts an outward pressure to keep the wall in its original position. If the fingers are kept crooked whenever possible they have more strength than when extended.**

3. **The first pull continues as both hands move upward in one slow motion, exerting the same pressure as when the roll of clay was formed. Working slowly prevents deep ridges from forming; these weaken the wall and make successive pulls difficult. To prevent the roll of clay from peeling off the outside wall, it is grasped by the forefinger and forced inward and toward the top. As the roll is moved upward by the right hand, the pot grows taller.**

4. The raising process continues as another roll of clay is formed and pulled up in the same manner. The cross-section shows the position of the inside middle finger opposing the inward pressure of the right. If too much outward pressure is exerted, the shape will flare. When the wall rises straight from the bottom, the pressures of the two hands are correct. Note how the fingers of the two hands touch one another for continued support.

5. The cylinder may tend to spread at the top. This usually results from relaxing the hand pressures and surrendering to centrifugal force at the end of a pull. The wall can be brought back to a vertical position by encircling the bottom of the piece with both hands and riding to the top, keeping the pressure of the hands exactly the same from bottom to top. This process, called constricting, and used constantly in the throwing processes.

6. An uneven rim means that the piece either wasn't properly centered or that uneven raising pressures caused the distortion. To cut off the unevenness, wheel speed is reduced to one and the clay is lubricated. The right hand, carefully supported, very slowly cuts through the top of the wall with a pointer. When the pointer is through the clay and touches the left hand finger riding opposite, it is raised to remove the clay ring.

7. The cylinder is completed when the wall seems to be of an even thickness from bottom to top and when the wall has been thinned as much as is desired. A smooth finish can be obtained by using a soft fine sponge on the outside, instead of the fingertips, on the last pull. The top of the rim should be sponged also. A still smoother finish can be obtained by using a wooden rib, instead of the sponge, on the final pull to finish the piece.

8. The finished pot is cut in half to reveal wall thickness. The slight thickening of the wall at the base is left to prevent distortion of the shape when it is cut and removed from the wheel head. Aside from the excess clay left for support, the wall thickness should be uniform. The beginner should cut through pots from time to time; only in this way can he be assured of having learned to coordinate sense of touch with sight.

MAKING A BOWL

Courtesy, The St. Paul Gallery and School of Fine Arts

STONEWARE BOWL by Karl Martz

Courtesy, The Detroit Institute of Arts

STONEWARE BOWL by Clyde Burt

MAKING THE BOWL, the second basic shape, presents the potter with some problems that differ from those encountered in forming the cylinder. The inside bottom of the bowl is rounded, with the wall being a continuation of its curve. This is in sharp contrast to the flat-bottomed cylinder which has its mass rising at a right angle to the base. Moreover, while height is generally desired in the cylindrical form, width is the more important element in the bowl.

The differences are dictated by the uses to which a bowl is put. Food may be served or eaten from a bowl, and for this purpose the rounded inside shape facilitates the use of a spoon. When the bowl is used to hold such things as fruit or flowers, width provides an attractive display of the contents. Since the bowl often is essentially decorative, meeting an aesthetic need, it should have an appealing rounded form that invites the viewer to lift and hold it.

Because of the unique requirement for the bowl shape, the potter must learn how to fulfill them. Unlike the cylinder, which depends largely upon the outside hand for its shaping, the bowl is formed primarily from the inside, with the left hand exerting most of the pressure and, thereby, determining the shape. Since the use of the *right hand* is more important for control in the cylinder, and the *left hand* equally important for shaping the bowl, it is apparent that the potter must be ambidextrous. In effect, he must be able to do the same things — alternately shaping and countering — with either hand and with equal ease. Consequently, the left-handed person has no more difficulties to overcome at the wheel than does the right-handed.

The first step in throwing a bowl — centering — is the same as that for the cylinder. The wheel is operated at speed *four* and the hands and clay are lubricated with water whenever needed. When centering is completed and checked, opening is begun. It is at this point that the potter departs from the procedure followed in making the cylinder.

BOWL by Mary Lindheim

1. An alternate method of opening is shown: the two thumbs are placed back-to-back for support instead of one on top of the other. For this technique to work successfully, the thumbs must be held rigidly together to avoid going off center. With the wheel at <u>speed three,</u> the thumbs find the exact center of the top of the lump and carefully press straight down to the desired depth.

2. The first variation in making the bowl shape comes in opening. After the thumbs press down to open the lump, they push <u>up and out</u> to form an uninterrupted curve from bottom center to the rim. The beginner must avoid forming an angle in the bottom! The spreading motion of opening is repeated several times, starting at the center each time, to enlarge the inside diameter.

3. The cross-section shows the inside opening when it is completed and before the wall is raised. Note the uninterrupted curve: this is the shape desired for the finished bowl. From this point on, most of the potter's problems are concerned with maintaining the rounded inside line while extending the width of the bowl. Each operation must be tested for centering.

4. Excess clay is brought up from the outside bottom with the knuckle or middle finger of the right hand. The inside hand starts from the center, and rides up lightly until the two working fingers are opposite. Then both come up together. After this first pull, the inside hand exerts more pressure than the outside hand — just the reverse of the hand pressures in the cylinder method.

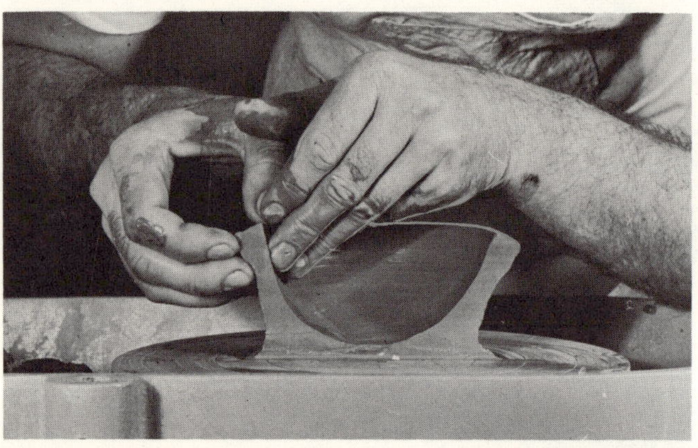

5. The inside fingers enlarge and control the shape, as is shown in the cross-section. The outside fingers act as a countercheck to keep the shape from expanding more than desired. The clay wall at the rim is left slightly thicker than the wall under it as the shape progresses; added width of the pot comes from the clay left there to expand the diameter of the bowl. Wheel speed is <u>two</u>.

7. Inside shape and wall thickness are revealed in the cross section. Excess clay left at the outside base supports the wall against sagging while it is being expanded. It also gives support later when the bowl is lifted from the wheel. Excess clay is tooled away during the foot-rimming process. When the potter can pull up a bowl quickly and surely, the amount left for support can be reduced.

6. The final pulls are made with the hands interlocked for support and the wheel moving at <u>speed one</u>. Pot width grows as a result of more pressure outward with the inside fingers; the pads of the fingers extend the excess clay at the rim into width. Excess throwing water must be sponged from inside the pot frequently to prevent the shape from sagging or collapsing.

Courtesy, The Detroit Institute of Arts

BOWL by Roy Pederson

Courtesy, The Brooklyn Museum

EARTHENWARE BOWL by Edwin Scheier

LIFTING FROM THE WHEEL

WHEN A PIECE is to be saved and finished with a foot rim, it must be removed from the wheel and put aside to stiffen before work can be continued. After the piece is thrown, and while the wheel is rotated, the throwing water is swabbed from its inside and the pot is allowed to dry for a short time.

If a pot becomes very water-soaked from a prolonged working time or has a flaring shape like a bowl, it is more likely to distort when moved from the wheel. Depending on the condition of the clay and the shape of the piece, a pot may be removed from ten to thirty minutes after it has been made.

Special tools the potter needs for this process are a cutting wire to sever the base of the pot from the wheel and a pair of lifters to remove it. The *cutting wire* is fashioned from any very thin, flexible cord or wire; its length is about equal to the wheel head diameter. *Lifters* are fashioned from any sturdy metal that won't bend under the weight of the pots; the shape illustrated is convenient to handle. A pair of pancake turners can be used for lifters. The potter also needs *bisque tiles*, *plaster bats* or *masonite squares* on which to place pots when they have been lifted.

1. The wheel is rotated, counter-clockwise, at <u>speed one</u>. A handful of water is splashed at the pot's base to lubricate the cutting wire. The wire is stretched taut across the wheel on the far side of the piece, then slowly pulled straight toward the potter through the clay base.

2. This process is repeated, again splashing water at the base before cutting. The wire must be held tightly; if the potter relaxes his hold during this process, it may slash into the wall and ruin it. The potter must resist the urge to move his hands in the direction of the moving wheel.

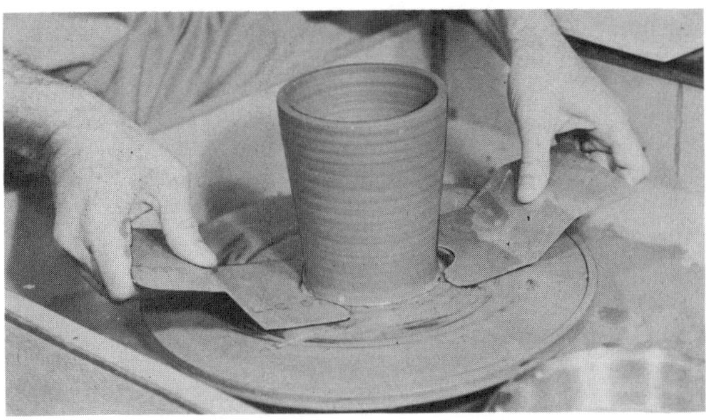

3. The wheel now is stopped. The pair of lifters is held in the hands and the front, or working ends are dipped into water for lubrication. They are gently pushed under the base from opposite sides as far as they will go without being forced. Now the wheel is rotated <u>slowly</u>.

4. The lifters are held very firmly; as in the case of the cutting wire, the potter must guard against surrendering his hands to the rotating movement of the wheel head. The lifters now are slowly and carefully pushed on under the center of the pot until their tips touch one another.

5. The pot is raised on the lifters from the moving wheel head and set on a tile. The lifters, held at a slight downward angle to the center, are gently pulled from under the pot. If one lifter sticks, a finger is held against that side of the pot while it is being removed.

FOOT RIMMING THE CYLINDER

THE TYPE OF FOOT treatment used for pottery varies with the individual potter. Some potters prefer not to make a foot at all, but merely to cut the pot from the wheel and consider it finished. Others tool little more than a slightly concave bottom. Many prefer a more formal foot treatment.

Learning to cut the foot rim on the thrown pot is as important as mastering throwing itself. A poorly designed, raggedly cut foot can ruin an otherwise handsome shape. Properly made, the foot gives "lift" to a piece of pottery, producing a delicate and graceful appearance and preventing the pot from appearing "table bound."

Functionally, the foot can prevent damage to the pot since it is better able to absorb shock than is a broad, flat surface. It also can protect the surface on which the pot is placed.

Formal treatment falls into two different categories—the visible and the hidden foot. A visible foot is one that is seen when the piece is viewed in its normal, upright position. The hidden, or invisible, foot doesn't interrupt the contour or profile of the pot and can be seen only when the piece is inverted.

There are no hard-and-fast rules concerning the use of either type. Generally, the visible foot is used on bowls and the hidden one on cylindrical forms. The potter must study the pot he has made and then decide which foot style will best continue or contrast with its shape for the effect he has in mind. In order to achieve harmonious results, the relationship of the height and width of a visible foot to the shape it supports is one of the potter's most important considerations.

The potter can learn to make the right choice in selecting foot rim styles for his work by observing the results of the work of others and studying all available pictures of pottery to decide whether foot treatment is successful and, if not, how it could be improved. It is equally important for the potter to throw and foot rim as many pots as possible and evaluate each result.

Cutting foot rims is not difficult to learn, but beginners should not save pots expressly to foot rim them until their work is true. If a pot is not round or has an uneven rim, footing can be made most difficult. But when a satisfactory piece has been made, it is lifted from the wheel and set aside in a damp box for slow drying. The pot is ready for foot rimming when it is leather-hard—that is, just stiff enough to be handled without deforming.

Good turning tools are extremely important. The cutting ends should be firm, since those that are flexible, such as wire-end tools, tend to chatter and produce an uneven surface. Thin steel cutting blades, sharp on both edges, are best. To provide a secure grip and better control, handle lengths should be from six to ten inches. It is advisable to have a round-end tool for cutting away and a flat-end tool for finishing.

1. The rim of the piece to be footed must be round. If the rim has become distorted upon being lifted from the wheel or during drying in the damp box, it can be re-shaped at this stage of leather-hardness. A slick-surfaced container, such as a metal or glazed bowl or pan, is used for this process. It must relate to the shape of the pot to be reshaped — smaller at the base and wider at the rim. It is pressed gently inside the rim of the clay piece and is rotated until the rim is round.

2. The thickness of the base must be measured to determine how deep a foot rim can be cut. A stick is laid across the rim, its ends extending beyond the edges of the pot. Another stick is held upright on the <u>outside</u>, and marked with a pencil where the horizontal piece crosses it. The process is repeated, this time with the vertical stick held <u>inside</u> the pot, and standing on the lowest inside area. The distance between the two pencil marks is the thickness of the base of the pot at its <u>thinnest point</u>.

3. The piece is inverted on the wheel head and centered. The concentric circles inscribed on most wheels are helpful as guides for centering but are not accurate enough for this precision work. The arms and hands are firmly braced, and a pencil or pointer is brought in toward the pot on the slow-moving wheel until the pencil just touches the pot at the lowest point where tooling is desired.

4. The wheel is stopped and the pot moved very carefully away from the marked side. This procedure is repeated until the pencil touches the pot all the way around and the pot is centered. If the pointer touches only on two opposite sides, the pot is not quite true, and this is as close as it will come to being centered. Coils or "keys" of clay are firmly pressed against the pot to secure it to the wheel.

5. Tooling is begun with the wheel rotating at a slow speed. The round-end tool is carefully and firmly brought down on the bottom of the pot just slightly away from the center. It bites into the clay, taking off only a slight amount, as it slowly spirals across the surface outward to obtain a smooth, flat surface. The small nub left in the center is a reminder of how much clay has been removed.

6. The outside of the pot is tooled to remove the excess clay left in the bottom for support. Starting from above, the rigidly held round-end tool is spiraled down to remove the excess clay. Only a small amount of clay is removed at a time; an attempt to remove too much might result in a gouge that could ruin the pot. This procedure is repeated to achieve the desired wall thickness.

7. The excess clay in the bottom is now tooled away to form the foot rim. A hidden foot is selected for this cylinder form. The stick indicating the bottom thickness is referred to again and checked in reference to the clay nub; it is a reminder of how much clay remains to be cut away. The footing tool is spiraled outward from the nub and stopped short of the edge to allow for foot rim width.

8. The cutting-away process is repeated until the excess clay is removed, after which a bottom wall thickness equal to the thickness of the side walls is left. The foot rim width also should equal the wall thickness measurement.

The flat-edge cutting tool is used, spiraling out from the nub, to level the surface and to square the corner at the rim. It also levels the foot itself and insures a flat base.

9. Finally, the nub is removed by spiraling the flat cutting tool toward the center. Throughout the footing process, it is essential that the tools be held rigidly and with the utmost control. The hands must be supported always, and the support board raised and lowered in order to keep the hands above the area being tooled. Working downward with the tools allows the hands better support.

10. As the wheel is revolved slowly, the pot is lightly sponged to give it a smooth finish and remove any clay burrs left from the cutting. The clay keys are carefully removed and the pot lifted from the wheel. If it feels heavier than it looks, it should be returned to the wheel for more tooling away of excess clay. The finished pot is returned to the damp box for slow drying.

FOOT RIMMING THE BOWL

THE PROCESS used in foot rimming the bowl is basically the same as that used in foot rimming the cylinder shape. Because of the extra clay left to support the wall, more excess clay must be tooled away if the weight of the piece is to be satisfactory. It is probable that the bowl will be given a visible foot, and this style offers more variation than the hidden foot treatment used on the cylinder.

The sketch shows some of the variations that the beginner may want to try. In A, the surface within the foot is convex, making the wall of the pot a continuous curve inside and out, broken only by the addition of the foot rim. B shows a concave surface inside the foot which forms a curve opposite to that of the inside of the bowl. C is a splay foot flaring at the bottom, with a flat surface treatment inside. D shows the hidden foot treatment with a concave surface on the inside of the rim.

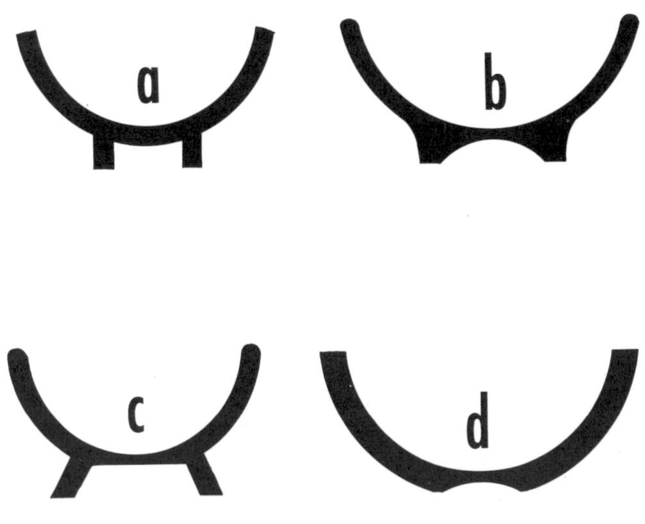

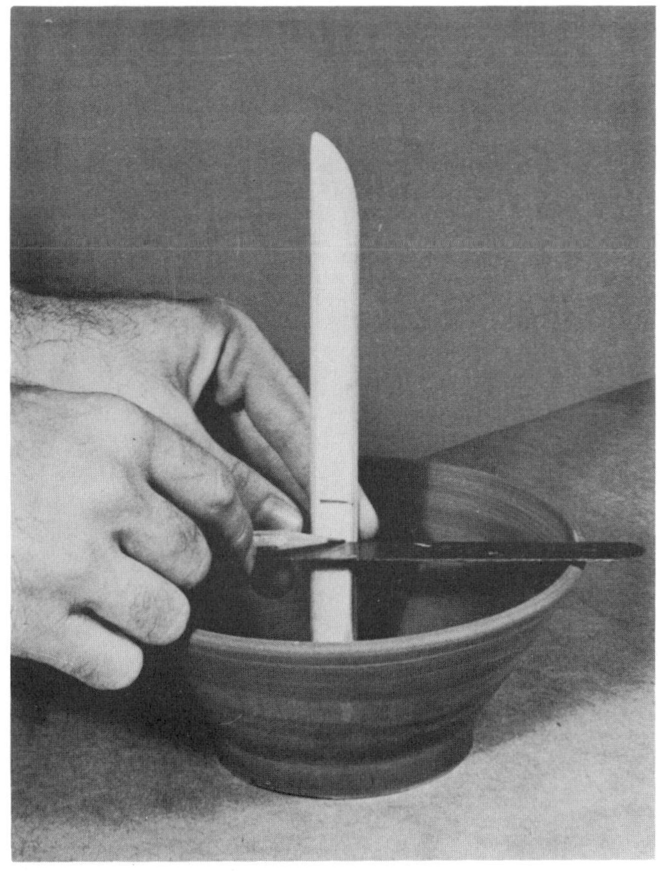

1. Bowl is measured for bottom thickness before being inverted on wheel head.

2. Pot is centered on wheel before being fastened with clay coils or keys.

3. Nub of clay is left in the center when bottom surface is leveled by tooling.

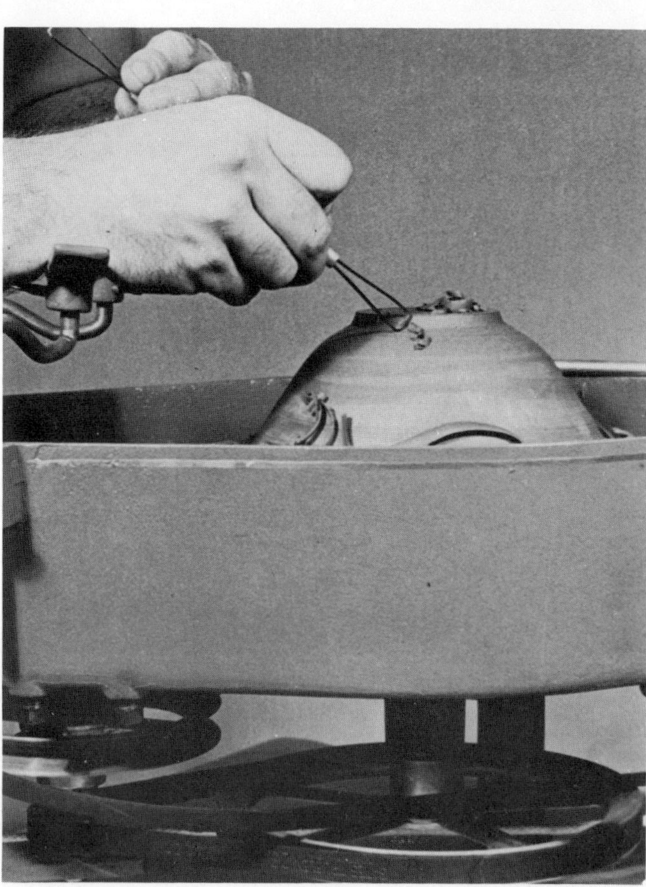

5. Visible foot rim is established on bowl's contour after support clay is cut away.

4. Foot rim diameter is decided and excess clay is cut from the bottom wall.

6. Foot rim is tooled on inside. Foot style is similar to A in the sketch.

THROWING ON TILES AND BATS

CERTAIN SHAPES, particularly bowls or pots that flare out at the top, can be easily distorted if they are cut from the wheel head and removed with lifters. This problem can be minimized if the pot is allowed to stiffen on the wheel before being removed. However, this prevents the potter from using his wheel again immediately. To eliminate this "waiting period," many potters throw these shapes on tiles or bats.

There are many advantages in using tiles and bats. They are easily attached to the wheel head and they hold securely, yet are easy to remove. Tiles are inexpensive and readily available. Plaster bats are easily made in pie pans. Since thin bats and tiles present virtually no storage problem, enough can be kept on hand so there never is any danger of running short.

Some wheels have recessed throwing heads, and *all* throwing is done on plaster bats that fit inside. Other wheels have reversible wheel heads. When these are upright, the throwing is done on the wheel head; when reversed, the potter works on plaster bats that fit inside the throwing ring.

On standard, non-reversible metal wheel heads, plaster bats can be attached by smearing the bottoms of the bats with a large quantity of thick slip. The bottom is immediately pressed down on the dry wheel head and held until the bat is firmly attached.

When the pot is thrown, the bat or tile is lifted from the wheel by prying up a corner or section with a flat, rigid blade. When the leather-hard pot is ready for foot rimming, it can be cut from the tile with a wire or a fettling knife. Pots thrown on plaster bats release themselves at this stage. After the used tiles or bats are cleaned, they are allowed to dry before being used again.

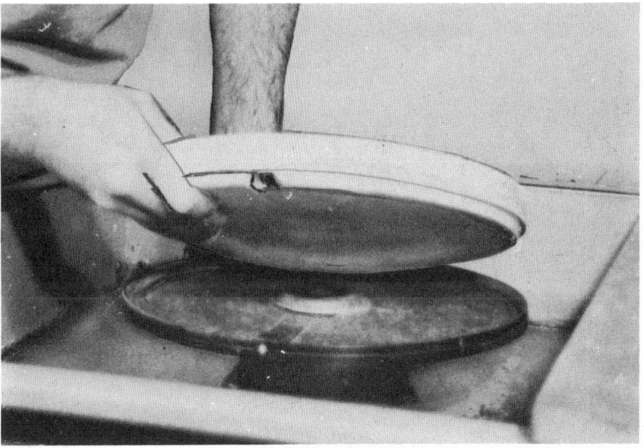

1. Reversible wheel head is inset to hold plaster bats on which the potter does his throwing.

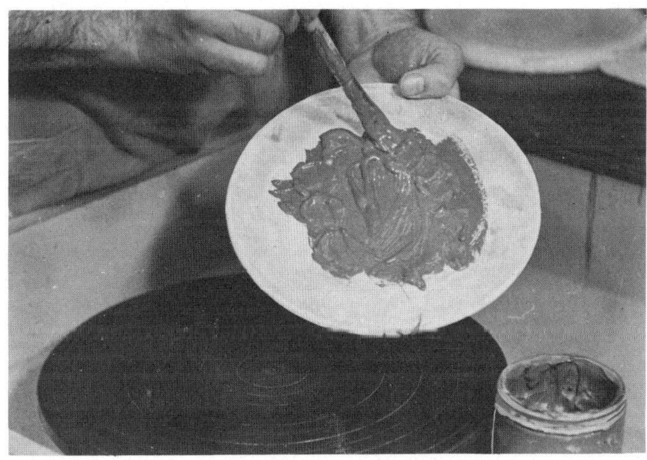

2. A dry plaster bat is attached to the wheel head by smearing thick slip heavily onto the bottom of the bat.

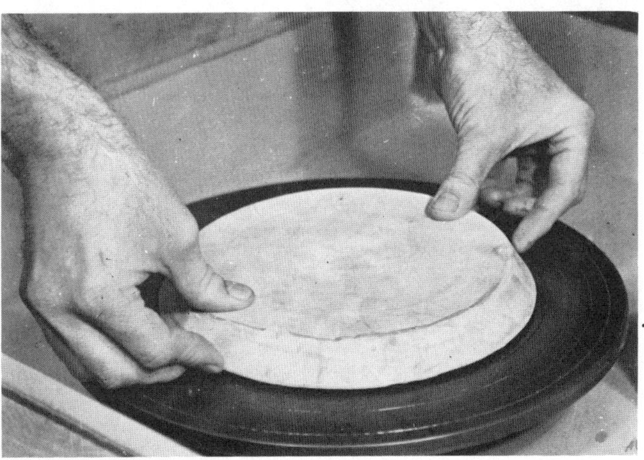

3. The bat is immediately pressed down on the wheel head and held firmly until it is solidly attached.

4. A quantity of thick slip is brushed on the back of a dry, unglazed tile. If the tile has raised ridges on its back, the slip is brushed on these areas.

5. While the slip still is wet, the tile is immediately placed on the wheel, slip side down. In a matter of seconds the tile "freezes" in place.

6. A small coil of clay is used to seal the sides of the tile against the wheel head, to prevent throwing water from seeping under and undermining the tile.

7. The surface of the tile is dampened by sponging water on the center. When the water disappears into the surface, the lump of clay is thrown onto the tile.

8. A gentle pressure is used in the preliminary stages of centering the clay. If the clay is approached too roughly, the tile may be forced from the wheel.

3

SPECIFIC SHAPES

JARS AND VASES

WHEN THE POTTER has learned the basic throwing steps of centering, opening, pulling up cylinders and bowls, and tooling the foot rims, he is ready to make the specific shapes that evolve from these fundamentals of wheel work.

Jars and vases constitute the greatest number of pieces made on the potter's wheel. The reason for their popularity with potters may be that they present uncomplicated shapes that are ideal for the use of decoration and unusual glaze effects.

Among the specific shapes, jars and vases are presented first because the student potter will find these shapes good for practice purposes after mastering the cylinder. They are almost direct outgrowths of the cylinder, since they emphasize height rather than width and generally are vertical in wall shape. Also, they are an incentive to the student to use larger amounts of clay for producing taller shapes and bigger pots.

In addition, making these vertical forms gives the potter a chance to experiment and practice foot rim treatment in relation to a specific form. Here also is a good project for investigating the effects of weak, strong, or eradicated throwing rings (marks from the contact of the fingers with the clay). And, of course, the most valuable experience of all is in learning even more control of the clay and the potter's wheel.

Shaping the piece from the basic cylinder form is the primary problem in making a vase or jar. In drawing up the straight cylinder, the pressure of both hands is nearly equal. However, in defining the form for a vase, one hand exerts more pressure and is largely responsible for the resulting shape.

Shaping is done by alternately pressing *out* with the inside hand to enlarge the form, and *in* with the outside hand to narrow the shape. The hands must cooperate: while one hand is concerned with the shaping process, the other supports and guides. This process prevents the shaping hand from exerting too much pressure and possibly distorting the form.

In pulling up the basic cylinder from which the vase is to be made, the potter must keep in mind the shape he wants to make. Where the shape is to swell out, some extra clay must be left in that part of the wall area; otherwise, the wall will be too thin in that place. Shaping *thins* the wall, and clay cannot be brought up from a thicker wall area to fill a thinner section. And when any area becomes too thin for the rest of the wall, there is danger of the pot collapsing.

Courtesy, The Cranbrook Foundation

VASE by Maija Grotell

LARGE JAR by Karl Martz

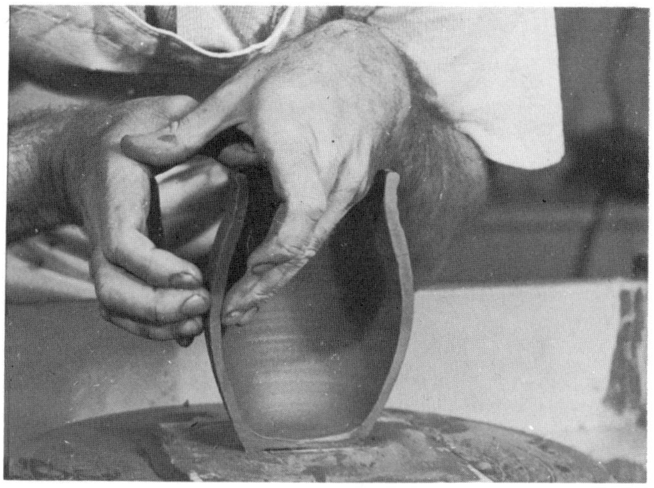

1. To enlarge the width of the cylinder for shaping, the inside hand exerts more <u>outward</u> pressure than for the straight-up-and-down form. The outside hand's counter pressure follows the curve being described from the inside.

2. The form is narrowed at the top by more <u>inward</u> pressure from the right hand working on the outside. Both hands move at the same distance from each other at all times to maintain an even wall thickness for the vase shape.

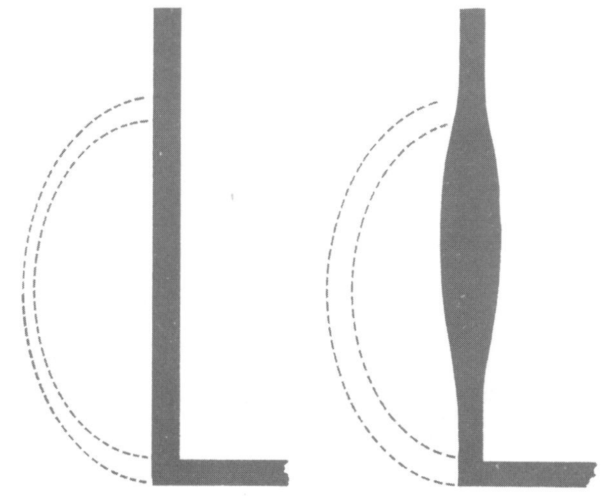

3. The cylinder wall must be left thicker at any area where the potter intends the shape to swell or bulge. Any outward shaping makes the wall thinner, and too much variation in wall thickness may cause the pot to collapse.

STONEWARE VASE by F. Carlton Ball

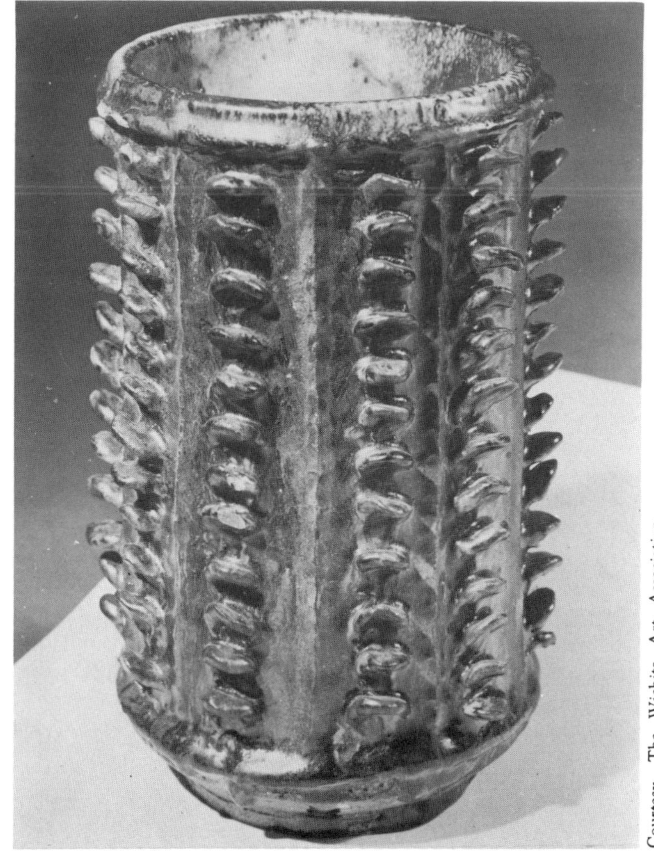

STONEWARE VASE by Henry H. Lin

Courtesy, The Wichita Art Association

33

PITCHERS

MAKING A PITCHER involves not only the techniques of throwing and shaping a cylinder and cutting its foot rim (all of which have been discussed in previous sections), but also the new problems of forming a pouring spout and making and applying a handle.

A good pitcher must have a spout that will *pour* and a handle that will *lift* and *balance* the pot. The pouring spout, which is formed at the rim of the plastic pot, must be wide enough to channel the liquid through it, and it should be drip-proof. Generally, a spout that levels out horizontally and then turns abruptly down, coming to a sharp edge, is least likely to drip.

A pulled handle is usually considered the best complement to a thrown shape, since it most successfully retains the plastic character of clay.

The problem of relating the handle to the shape must be given special consideration; the handle should be neither too heavy nor too slight for the size and character of the pitcher. It isn't always easy for the potter to provide a handle which gives proper lifting balance and is, at the same time, aesthetically an integral part of the pitcher.

The technical aspects of combining separate elements to form a pitcher can be learned quickly, but making a successful pitcher requires much experimentation and observation. The beginner should examine a variety of pitchers. When he sees a spout that pours well, he should discover why. He should lift pitchers, both empty and full, to discover whether the handles balance and function. If he thinks that any part of a pitcher is good, he should try to incorporate it in his work. By the same token, if pieces do not please him, he should try to isolate the offending features and avoid them in his work.

PITCHER by Dean Strawn

PITCHER by Angelo Garzio

Courtesy, The Tweed Gallery

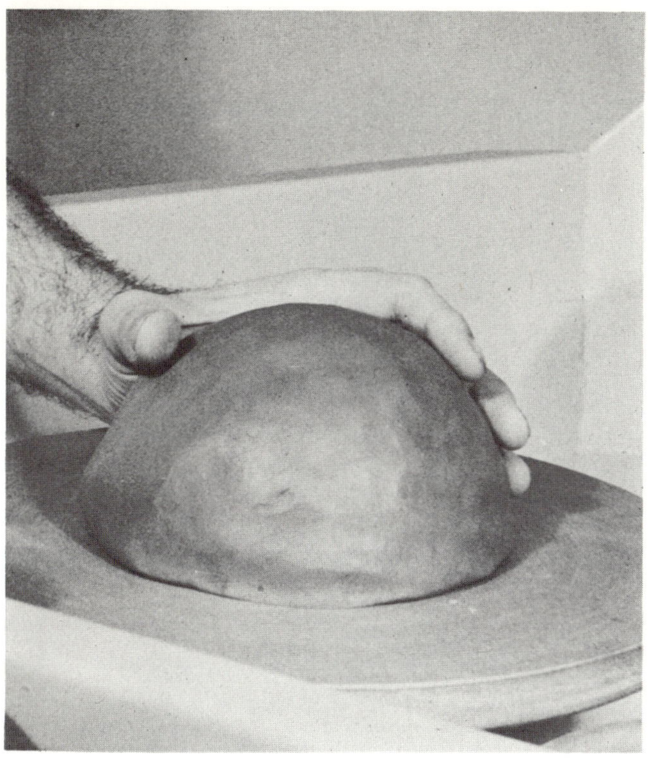

1. The pitcher presented here is a good shape for beginners to attempt since it makes use of a basic form similar to that demonstrated for the vase and jar project, and thus presents no new problems in the shaping process. The lump of clay on the wheel head shows the amount of well-wedged clay needed to raise a pitcher of this size.

3. When the cylinder has been swelled out for the pitcher shape, the neck is constricted to complete the form. This is done by encircling the pot with both hands and gradually applying pressure as the hands approach the area to be narrowed. Wrinkles that form are removed by pulling up the wall after each constricting process.

2. The lump of clay is centered, opened and pulled up into a cylinder. The bracket shows where the lower midsection of the wall is left thicker to provide the extra clay necessary for swelling out the finished pitcher shape. If this is not done, the wall will be too thin when the clay is stretched and very likely might collapse or deform.

4. The pouring spout is formed after the pitcher is formed and the wheel is stopped. The thumb and forefinger of the left hand support the outside rim, pushing in very gently, while the right hand forefinger gently pulls the spout out from the inside. Both hands start well down the wall and increase pressure as they approach the top.

5. The inside finger pressure is a gentle, stroking action. The outside fingers act as a counter-pressure to prevent the rim being distorted from within. If pressure from either hand is too strong or abrupt, the rim may crack. Fingers must be kept lubricated. The spout is completed by being pulled directly out, horizontally, and the end shaped down.

6. The completed pitcher shape is cut free of the wheel head with a wire, then is lifted on a pair of dampened metal lifters and placed on a tile. After slow drying to the leather hard stage in the damp box, it is returned to the wheel, inverted and its foot rim is tooled. An invisible, or hidden, foot treatment is used on this cylindrical form.

WINE PITCHER by Doris Jean Strachen

STONEWARE PITCHER by Harvey K. Littleton

Courtesy, The Museum of Contemporary Crafts

MAKING A PULLED HANDLE

THE HANDLE is such an important part of many shapes that it must be considered as an essential part of the potter's craft. It may be hand-built, wheel-thrown or made of a material other than clay. The *pulled* handle, however, seems best to complement the thrown shape since it best retains the plastic quality.

In making a pulled handle, the clay is *pulled down* from a lump of wedged clay with a hand pressure similar to that used in milking a cow. As the clay is pulled down, it is shaped in the hand to the desired length, width and thickness. The action of the fingers on the wet clay gives pulled handles the same plastic quality that characterizes wheel-thrown pottery.

Like milking a cow, pulling a handle is not a technique that one masters the first time it is tried. With a little practice, though, the potter soon finds that it is not difficult to do and that it is one of the most satisfactory ways to make handles for his pottery.

Gaining proficiency at pulling the handle is only part of the potter's work. He must be able to make a handle which will perform its task in relation to any given shape. Since it must provide lift and enhance its beauty, the potter must make sure that the handle is neither too heavy nor too slight for the size and character of the pot for which it is intended.

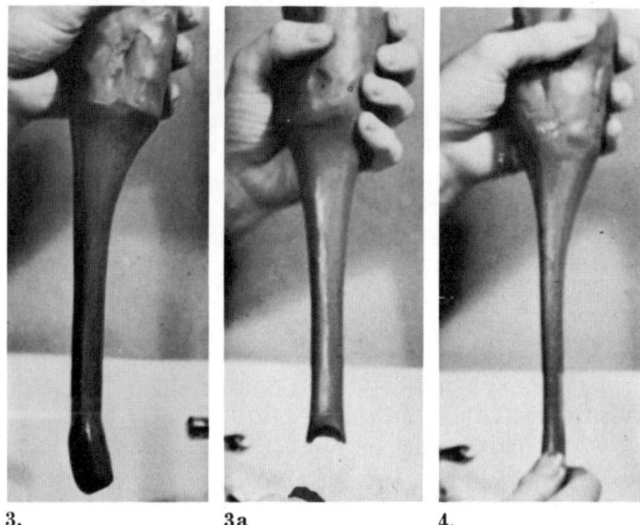

3. 3a 4.

3. If a thick lump of clay develops at the bottom at any time during the pulling processes, it is pinched off and discarded. If this is left on, it can cause the upper portion to be distorted during successive pulls. More clay is pulled down from the lump top to replace this discarded portion if extra length is needed.

4. When the general size of handle has been pulled down, its shape is defined. The right hand thumb and forefinger, held opposite each other, carefully pull down to flatten the shape. Occasionally, the handle is turned around to work on the reverse side, and a few strokes are given the sides to keep them straight and true.

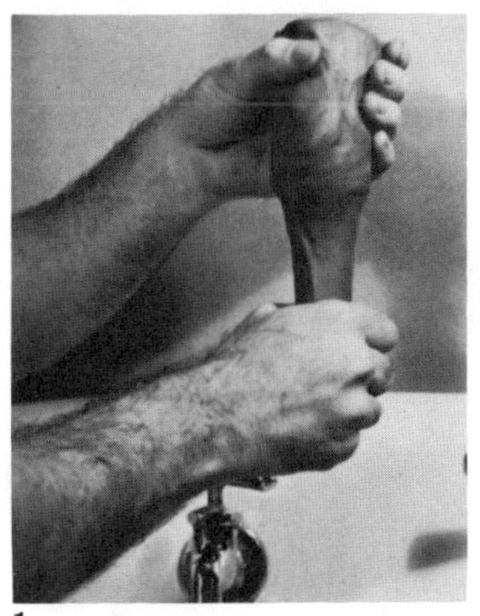

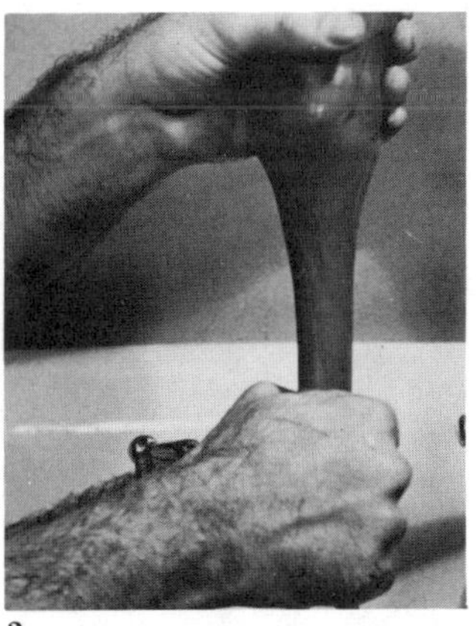

1. 2.

1. A piece of well-wedged clay is shaped into a thick, stubby coil. This is grasped at the top by the left hand, which supports it while it is formed into a handle. The right hand, well-lubricated with water, grasps the lower section of the coil and squeezes it lightly as it pulls downward to form a thick strand.

2. This same pulling action is repeated to lengthen the strand of clay. The right hand always returns to the main lump of clay to start a new stroke, pulling more of the clay down. The lump is turned occasionally to insure a well-balanced, round shape that tapers toward the bottom. The pressure must be gentle to avoid tearing the strand.

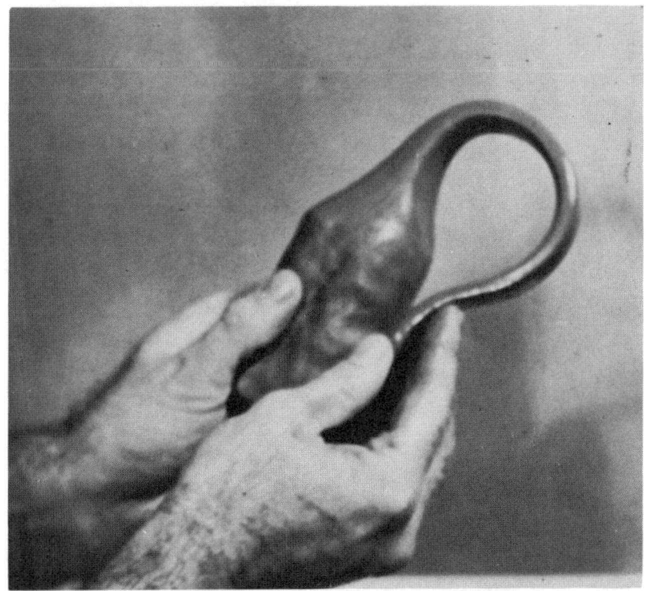

5. After the handle is shaped to the desired length, width and thickness, the bottom is bent over to meet the lump. A light pressure fastens them together to hold the handle in position while it firms up. When it is stiff enough to be handled without losing its shape (usually from 10 to 20 minutes) it is attached to the pot.

ATTACHING THE HANDLE

THE HANDLE usually is pulled immediately after the pot has been foot rimmed. While the handle is stiffening, the area on the pot where it is to attach is dampened with a sponge and covered with a damp cloth.

Some potters attach a handle soon after the pot is thrown — usually about an hour or so afterwards. Needless to say, this is difficult since the thrower must be able to work quickly and decisively in order to avoid deforming the soft pot. The beginner will find the method demonstrated here easier and more suited to his early skills.

Attaching the handle requires not only the skill to get it on the pot, but also the ability to place it where it will function best and complement the general design.

A handle may be attached so that it appears to "grow-out" of the pot, much as a limb grows from the trunk of a tree. Another type of joining is more abrupt, with a "stuck-on" appearance. These two treatments also may be combined, with the handle appearing to grow out of the pot where it joins at the top and attaching more or less lightly at the tail.

The placement of the handle in relation to the shape is quite important. The beginner must remember to be aware of the inside profile created by the space between the pot and handle. This negative shape must please the eye just as much as the outside profile of the handle on the pot.

1. The handle is made immediately after the pot has been foot rimmed. While the handle is becoming firm enough to hold its shape, the area on the pot where it is to be attached is dampened and covered with a damp cloth to retain the moisture. There is less chance of the handle cracking off during the drying stage if this is done. An extra handle can be made in case one is not satisfactory.

2. The handle is pinched off the lump just where it begins to thin out. This provides the top portion with some extra size for a "growing out" appearance. It also is useful for welding clay from the handle into the pot area where it is to be attached. The handle is tried in several positions against the pot to determine where it will fit best. It must be exactly opposite the spout!

3. A pencil or stick is laid across the top of the pot to help line up the handle opposite to the spout. With its position on the pot determined, the areas where the handle is to be attached are marked. These places are scratched with a pointer or knife to assure a better weld between the pieces. The roughened areas next are dampened with some water or thick slip.

5. The bottom of the handle is attached by pressing the tail against the scored and dampened area on the pitcher. This joining, like the top one, can be well thumbed and integrated, or the handle may be attached lightly and casually at the tail. Notice how the right hand supports the inside of the pot against distortion from outside pressure during this attaching process.

4. The extra thickness at the top of the handle is blended into the body to integrate the parts. This gives the handle the sturdy appearance of "growing out" of the pot. As the excess clay is thumbed back and into the pitcher, the left hand supports the tail of the handle. The right hand fingers support <u>inside</u> the pitcher to keep the shape from being deformed by pressure from the outside.

6. If there isn't enough clay thickness in the handle where it attaches to the pot, small coils of plastic clay can be worked into these areas with the fingers or a wooden modeling tool. The joining areas next are smoothed with a fine sponge in the direction of the throwing marks; then the completed pitcher is set aside in the damp box to complete its drying slowly and safely.

BOTTLES

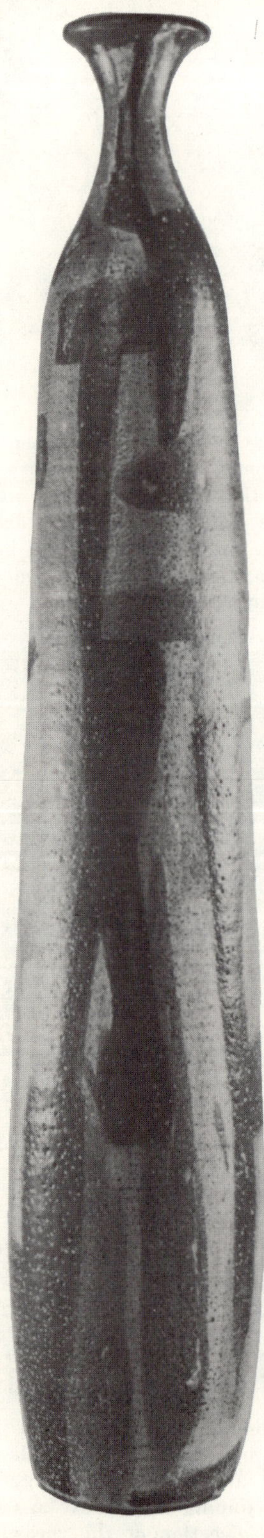

THE BOTTLE appears to be the most difficult shape to make on the potter's wheel, but this is not actually true. However, making a bottle *does* require more patience and more coaxing of the clay than do the simpler shapes encountered thus far.

A bottle is made by throwing a basic cylinder, shaping the lower section (the body of the bottle), and then constricting the upper section to form the shoulder and small neck.

The constricting process is quite involved, but the beginner on the wheel has had some experience in the process after having made the pitcher. Forming the neck of the bottle simply requires an extended use of the same constricting technique. After each constriction the wall is pulled up again, because the closing-in operation thickens the wall and often creates wrinkles. The counterplay of constricting and pulling up is repeated many times until the desired shape is achieved.

The first steps in making a bottle present no new problems. The clay is centered, opened and raised into a cylinder as for a vase or pitcher shape. The rim is not allowed to flare at any time during the pulling.

Courtesy, The M. H. DeYoung Memorial Museum

STONEWARE BOTTLE by Marc Hansen

PORCELAIN BOTTLE by Dale Hays

1. The cylinder wall is shaped to form the desired swell in the body, and then constriction of the top section is begun. The hands are very lightly placed around the wall at a point <u>below</u> the area where constricting is to begin; they move upward as their grasp tightens to narrow the shape. The forefingers ride above the other fingers, keeping the wall under control.

2. Constricting thickens and wrinkles the wall, and this area must be pulled up to thin and straighten it. The fingers are set slightly below the constricted section, both in and outside the pot, and move up with a slowly increasing pressure. During this process, the pressures between the fingers on the inside and those on the outside determine the shape of the shoulder.

3. The process of alternately constricting and pulling up the wall is repeated to narrow the neck and determine the final shape of the bottle. The ends of the fingers control the constricting as the neck is narrowed, and each attack is started far enough down to form and control the shoulder shape. The outside of the pot must be lubricated with water during constricting.

4. In pulling up the clay in the shoulder and neck after constricting, the potter must be careful not to thin the wall too much. The pulling-up process is done primarily to even the wall thickness and to help control the shape. If the wall is thinned too much, the shoulder may collapse or the neck may twist or even tear under the pressure of the potter's hands.

5. As the neck is made narrower, it becomes increasingly difficult to remove the water that accumulates inside the pot. A stick with a scrap of sponge fastened on one end is used to remove the water when the hand can no longer enter the opening with a sponge. The wheel must be rotating when the water is sponged out; otherwise, the inside of the pot may be damaged.

7. The rim is given a slight flare after the final constricting is done. The rim and the outside surface are sponged with an elephant ear or silk sponge to remove the dribbles of water from the throwing process, and the piece is cut from the wheel head, lifted from the wheel and set aside in the damp box to reach the leather-hard stage for foot rimming.

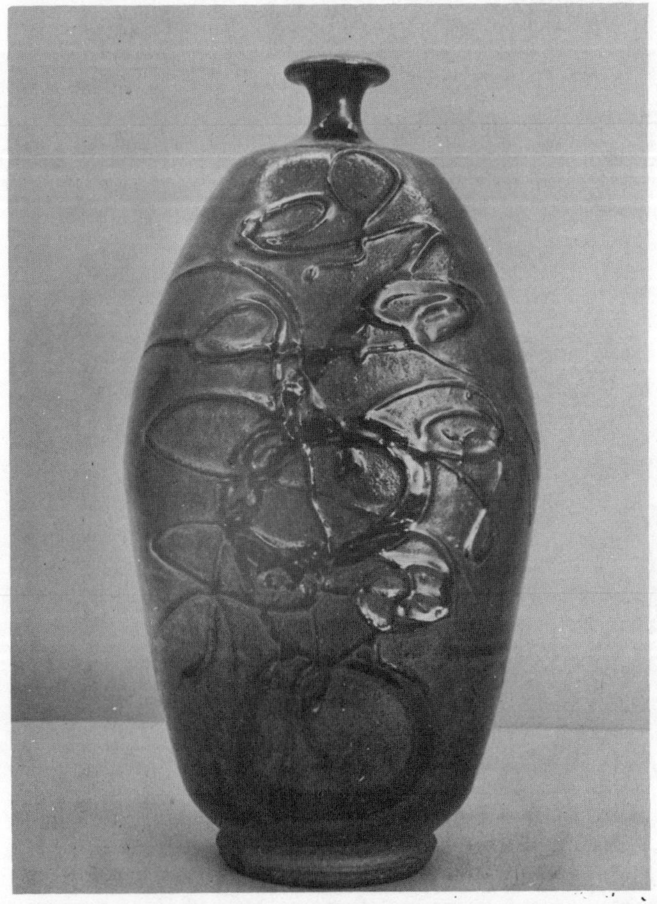

6. The wrinkles created in constricting, and the consequent variation in the thickness of the clay, result in an uneven top on the bottle after the pulling-up process. If this unevenness is allowed to remain, it may cause trouble during subsequent work on the neck. A small section at the rim should be removed with a pointer, leaving a level rim on the pot.

BOTTLE by Peter Voulkos   Courtesy, America House

FOOT RIMMING THE BOTTLE

FASTENING small-necked bottles upside down on the wheel for foot rimming is almost an impossibility, so the potter inverts them in a container called a *chuck* or cradle. This device is used to support the inverted pot by its shoulders, and to keep the mouth off the wheel. Although glass or pottery jars can be used for this purpose, they are apt to mar the leather-hard clay of the bottle where it contacts the sharp rim of the jar. The potter generally prefers to use a chuck made specifically for this job. Directions for making a chuck are given on page 44.

When the bottle is ready to be foot rimmed, its base is measured for depth in the usual manner. If the pot is very tall and its neck narrow, the stick used for measuring must, of course, be long and narrow — perhaps a length of small dowel rod may be used. With the measurement of the thickness marked, the pot is ready to be inverted in the chuck.

1. The bisque chuck is placed on the wheel head, approximately centered, and the bottle is inverted in it with the shoulder of the pot resting firmly in the flare of the chuck. The next step, leveling the base of the pot, can best be done by placing a small level on its bottom surface and adjusting the pot's position until the level shows it to be true. For an accurate reading, the level should be used in two positions at right angles to each other.

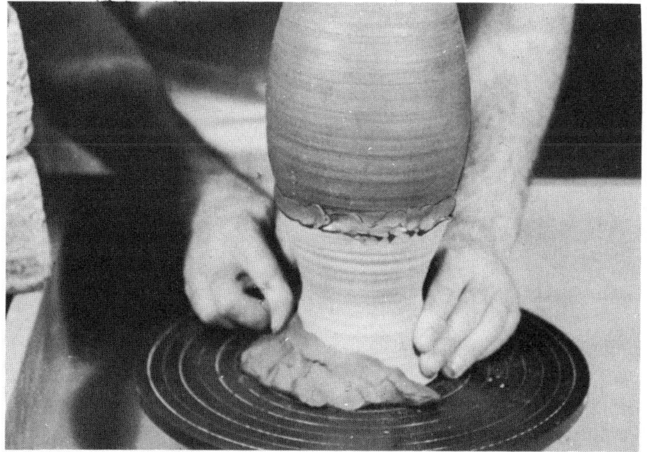

3. With the pot centered, the base of the chuck is dampened with water (to hold the clay coil more securely) and the chuck is keyed or fastened firmly to the wheel head with the clay coil. To center a bottle for foot rimming is a rather tedious process, and the student must be prepared to spend more time on this detail. During the tooling process of cutting the foot, he must proceed with great care because the chuck and pot structure is not a sturdy one.

2. When the pot is level, it is fastened in the chuck. The top area of the chuck is slightly dampened with the sponge; then a small coil of clay is pressed around the pot and chuck where they meet. The pot is held securely by the hands to avoid disturbing its position, and the coil is pressed in very gently. The pot and chuck are centered together by bringing a pencil in on the pot; the entire assembly is moved, by adjusting the chuck, until the pot is centered.

4. The foot rim is cut and any excess clay is trimmed from the bottom wall in the usual manner. The potter must use extreme care not to lose control of the cutting tool; a gouge can lift the bottle right out of the chuck. Taking small, careful bites with the cutting tool is the best way to avoid this. In order to have the hands supported above the working area, it may be necessary to elevate the arm-rest board by means of bricks or other devices.

MAKING A CHUCK

THE POTTER should have on hand several bisque chucks to use for foot rimming bottles on the wheel. These can be thrown easily and they furnish practice for the student in constricting a cylinder shape.

The height and shape of the bottles the individual makes will dictate the shapes of the chucks he needs; if he prefers to make long-necked shapes, he needs taller, longer chucks. However, if he has on hand a variety of chucks of different heights and widths, he will always find a comfortable and secure fit for a variety of bottle shapes.

Most potters prefer a chuck shaped like an hourglass, with each end a different size. This doubles the usefulness of the chuck, since it will fit bottles of two different sizes.

The chuck may be thrown directly on the wheel head or it may be thrown on a bat or tile. A bottom wall need not be left when the lump is opened, as this is later tooled out anyway to provide an opening in each end of the finished chuck. When the chuck is completely dry, it is bisque fired.

2. When the shape is leather hard it is inverted and returned to the wheel for finishing. When it has been centered and fastened, the bottom is cut out. This is done by holding the pointer at an angle inward and slowly cutting through the clay until the flat bottom is free of the sides. This section is lifted out and discarded, leaving both ends of the chuck open.

3. The rim must be tooled <u>level</u>; otherwise, the chuck will not rest securely on the wheel head when in use. The inside of the rim is beveled, tooled smooth and sponged. It is shaped this way to protect the shoulder of the bottle as it rests here during its trimming. The rim should be left slightly thicker than the rest of the wall to minimize warping during the firing.

1. Routine throwing techniques are used to make a chuck. A cylinder is raised and the desired hourglass shape is made by constricting. The hands press in as they move toward the center; then their pressure is released as they continue toward the top. The rim is flared, beveled slightly and smoothed with a sponge on the inside. The rim must be level!

IMPROVISING A CHUCK

BOTTLES WITH NECKS too long to be inverted into any available chuck can be foot rimmed by substituting a glass bottle or jar for the bisque chuck. This make-shift container must be tall enough to protect the neck and keep the rim of the bottle from touching the bottom of the glass jar, and it must have a neck opening of the proper size to support the shoulder of the leather-hard pot.

1. The glass jar chuck is used in exactly the same manner as is the bisque chuck. The bottle is inverted in it and leveled with the use of the small level. The clay pot is fastened to the rim of the glass container with a clay coil; softer clay is used for keys since the chuck is nonporous. After the bottle is centered, clay keys are used to secure the chuck to the wheel head.

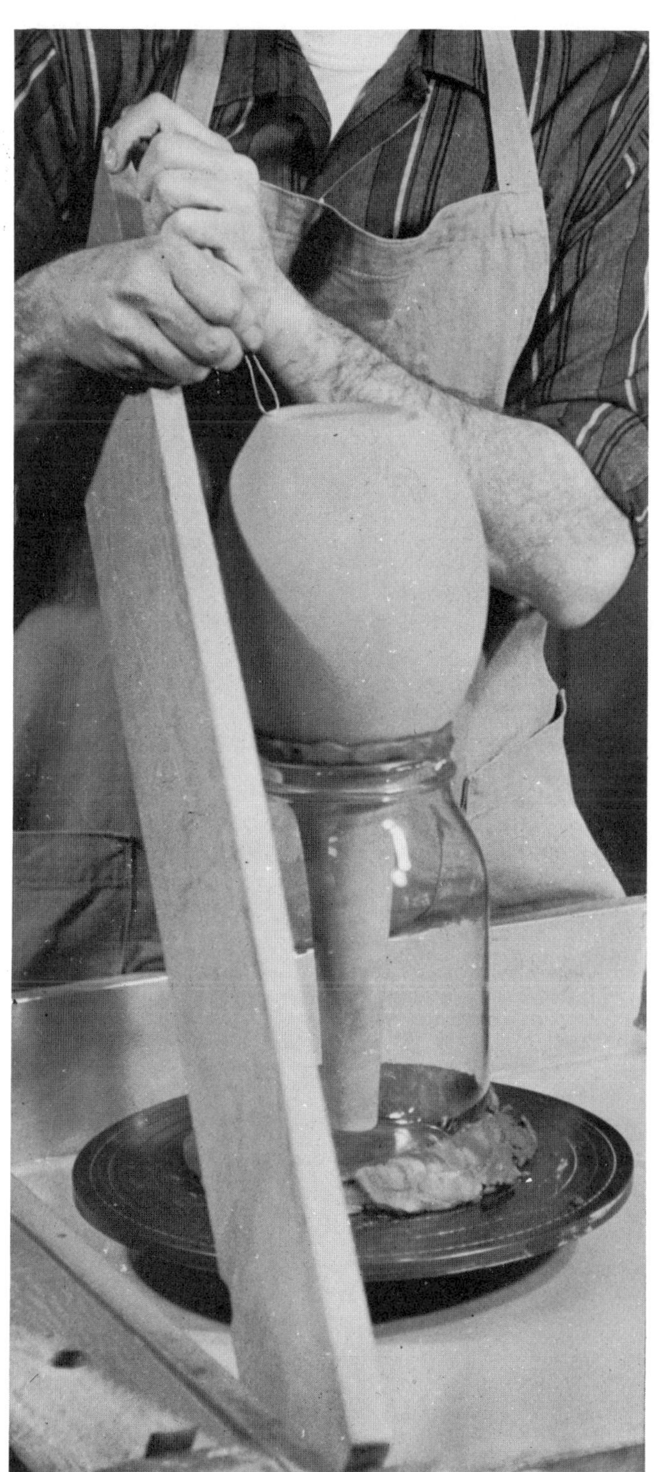

2. Foot rimming a pot in the glass chuck requires great care. The hands must be strongly supported and the tooling done slowly. A different method of support is illustrated. One end of the arm-rest board is braced against the well of the wheel and the other end under the potter's shoulder. The right hand supports itself against the edge of the angled board, which can be steadied in any direction.

COVERED JARS

THE ADDITION of a lid to a pot, like adding a handle, affects the character and may change the function of a piece. A lid must fit a pot in two ways. First, it must fit *physically*. Since its purpose is to close the container, it should fit snugly. Second, a lid must fit *aesthetically*. Because the lid may change or continue the shape of a container, the potter must concern himself with the flow of line between the pot and its lid.

There are various problems involved in making lids. Most lid types must be formed or shaped on the bottom as well as the top, which means that one part of the lid will be thrown and the other part tooled or trimmed after it has become leather hard. Lids may be thrown on the wheel either right side up or upside down; how it is done depends on the type of lid being made.

The three most used lids are the flat-inset lid, the curved-inset lid and the flanged lid.

The *flat-inset lid* is the easiest type of lid to make because it is thrown complete in one operation.

The *curved-inset lid* is thrown upside down. When it reaches the leather-hard stage, the knob is tooled from clay left in the base for that purpose.

The *flanged lid,* also thrown upside down and finished like the curved inset lid, is almost essential for shapes like the teapot and coffeepot: it won't fall out when the pot is tilted for serving.

There are many variations of these three basic lid types. And, with any of them, the tooled knob can be omitted and a pulled, coiled or other type

Courtesy, The Syracuse Museum of Fine Arts

COVERED JAR by Robert Turner

of hand-built knob can be substituted. On some lids, a knob isn't necessary at all.

In making lids, here are some points to keep well in mind:

1. Make the wall of the lid the same thickness as the wall of the pot.

2. When *adding* a knob to a lid, check proportions and style by working with the lid set on the pot.

3. Dry the lid and pot separately for faster drying. Bisque-fire the pot with the lid in place to prevent warping.

4. Allow for glaze thickness when measuring the lid for a tight fit.

5. When the flanged or curved lid is being glazed, the bottom rim (which corresponds to the foot rim on the pot) can be left unglazed to eliminate a stilting problem.

6. Pots can be glaze fired with their lids in place *only* if both areas of contact are left unglazed.

The treatment of the lip of the pot also must be considered when making a lid. Because the inside of the lid rests on the lip, it is an important detail. Sometimes the lip merely flares out, providing the lid with little more than a place to rest. This indefinite rim allows the pot to be used without its lid. Other lips have a definite groove (also called a ledge, ridge, seat or socket) into which the lid fits firmly. The advantage of the grooved lip is that it provides the lid with a closer fit.

SPHERICAL COVERED JAR by Peter Voulkos

Courtesy, The M. H. DeYoung Memorial Museum

COVERED PORCELAIN JAR

by Esther L. Beasley

Courtesy, The Joslyn Art Museum

PORCELAIN COVERED JAR

by Charles Lakofsky

Courtesy, The Syracuse Museum of Fine Arts

COVERED STONEWARE JAR

by James McKinnell

Courtesy, The Syracuse Museum of Fine Arts

COVERED URN by J. Sheldon Carey

FLAT-INSET LIDS

2. Accurate measurement of the opening is taken to make a lid of the proper dimension. A stiff piece of paper is laid across the top, and the inside diameter of the lip is marked on it with a pencil. The calipers are set to this measurement for use later.

1. The pot is thrown and given its final shaping on the wheel. Excess clay is left at the rim from which to form the groove into which the inset lid will fit. The groove is first formed with the fingers, then is defined more sharply by the use of a thin stick that is squared at the end.

3. After the pot is made and measured, it is removed from the wheel. Working on a tile or bat (see page 29), a small lump of clay is centered and flattened to a size slightly wider and higher than is desired for the finished lid. The calipers are kept nearby for measuring the width.

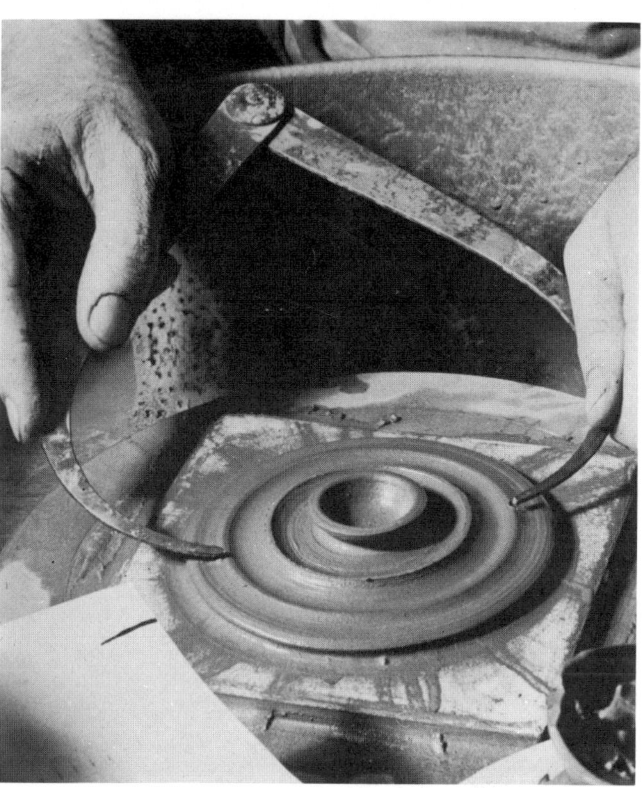

4. The excess height of clay is pressed toward the center, leaving only the thickness needed for the lid. The excess clay drawn toward the center is cut off with the pointer, but enough clay is left there from which to form a knob. The knob area clay is steadied by the left hand finger.

6. The pre-set calipers are set down across the lid, marking the desired diameter to fit the jar. The excess width is cut off by angling inward with the pointer so the edge of the lid will fit the angle of the groove. The finished lid remains on the tile until it releases itself.

Courtesy, The Museum of Contemporary Crafts

5. When the lid area has been leveled and evened, the knob is formed. The left forefinger opens the knob and rides inside while the right fingers gently pull the clay up into a wall. Excess clay pulled to the top is removed with a pointer when the final height is reached.

COVERED JAR by Robert Turner

CURVED-INSET LIDS

CASSEROLE by Floy Shaffer

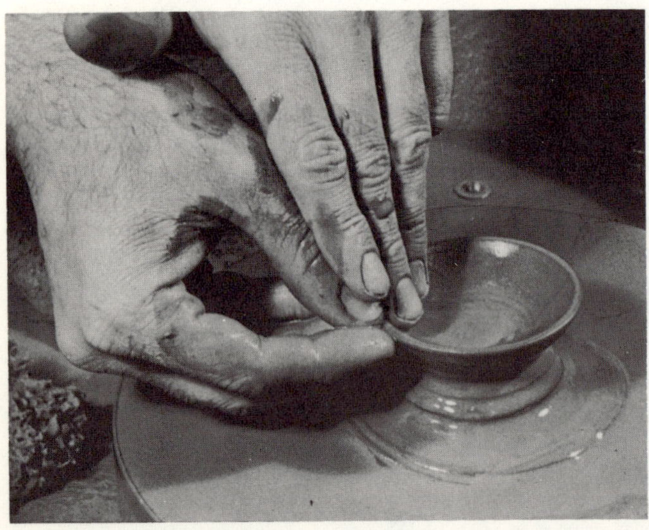

1. The curved inset lid is designed to fit rather loosely on a pot with a flaring rim. After the pot is thrown, its diameter is marked on a card and the calipers are set to this measure. The lid, thrown on a tile, is made like a bowl with excess clay left in the bottom for tooling a knob later on. Caliper measurements are used frequently to get the correct width for the lid.

3. The excess clay left in the base, except for the amount in the very center, is tooled away. This column of clay left in the center will become the knob, but this is not shaped until the rest of the tooling on the lid has been done. The thickness of the lid wall should be even from side to side, and should be the same thickness as the wall of the jar for which it is made.

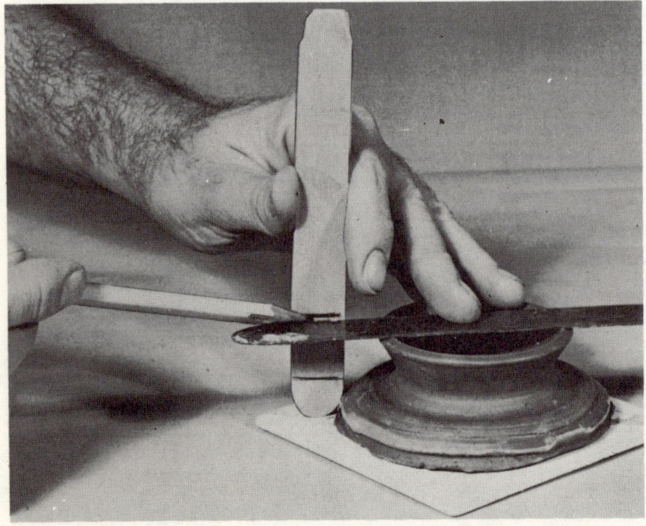

2. When the thrown lid is leather hard, the thickness of clay left in the base is measured to indicate the depth available for a knob. With a rigid stick across the top of the lid, the measurement to the inside bottom and to the outside bottom are taken on another stick. The lid is then cut from the tile, inverted and centered on the wheel head and fastened with small coils of clay.

4. The knob is shaped, the tooled area is sponged and the clay keys are carefully removed. This lid is among the most difficult ones for beginning potters because of the necessity of continuing the line of the pot in the lid. Too often lids made from the bowl shape are too high and call too much attention to themselves, instead of becoming part of an obvious whole.

FLANGED LIDS

1. The flanged lid maintains its position on the jar by means of a collar under the lid that fits inside the rim of the jar. This lid also is thrown upside down. The clay is centered, opened, and the wall raised in a cylinder. Excess clay is left in the base for tooling a knob later on. The "wall" is the flange; its height must be sufficient to hold the lid in place if the pot is tilted in use. This lid can be made to fit onto the top of a jar, or into a ledge. Two measurements are needed, the inside opening of the pot against which the flange fits, and the outside measurement of the rim or ledge which supports the lid on top of the pot.

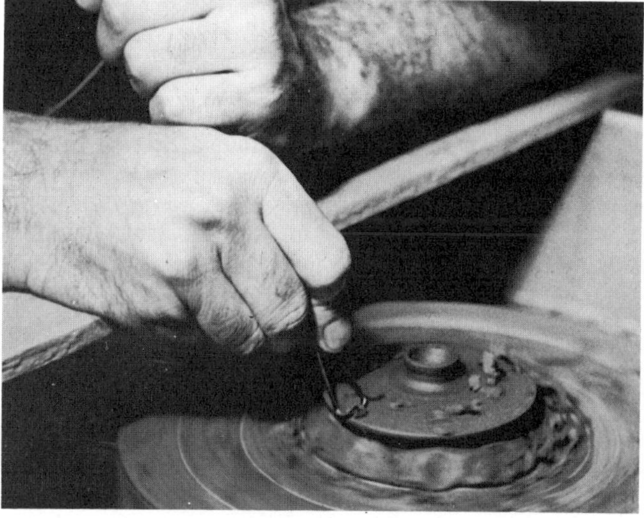

3. When the tooling of the top of the lid is complete, the knob is tooled. The center of the column is cut out first to make a hollow knob. Then the sides are tooled to correspond to the inner shape of the knob. After the lid is sponged, the clay keys are removed and the lid is set aside to dry.

2. When the lid is leather hard it is measured for the bottom thickness, then inverted and returned to the wheel and centered. It is fastened to the wheel head around its flange with clay keys. The excess clay is tooled away, again leaving the center column undisturbed.

COVERED JAR by Rex Mason

Courtesy, The Montreal Museum of Fine Arts

RECESSED-KNOB LIDS

THE RECESSED knob lid is rather unusual. This lid fits down into the top of its jar, and generally neither its wall nor its knob rises above the height of the jar wall.

The knob and wall are thrown in one operation, much like the flat inset lid, and there is a minimum of tooling required to finish it. The jar for which it is made must have a ledge to support the lid.

Two measurements are needed for this lid. The inside diameter of the mouth of the jar is measured on paper, and the calipers are set to this measure for use in making the lid. The depth of the ledge must be gauged if the lid is not to rise above the height of the jar. Much of the success of this type of lid lies in the accuracy of the measurements.

3. The knob is formed from the clay left in the center. This is done carefully to avoid tearing the small lump off its base. The height of both the knob and wall are carefully measured to insure their being no higher than the jar wall. When the piece is leather-hard it is inverted and returned to the wheel, where its underside is trimmed.

1.-2. A lump of clay is centered on a tile, and a depressed circle is formed by the fingers just off the center of the lump. The clay is pulled outward from this ridge, bringing it up between the two hands into a wall when the proper width is reached. If the wall becomes higher than desired, the excess clay is cut off.

ROSE-JAR LIDS

IN THE PAST this covered jar was widely used for preserving fragrant rose petals — hence its name.

The lid, which resembles an inverted small bowl, fits down closely over the neck of its jar. Because the lid fits on the top of the neck *and* on the shoulder of the jar, it achieves a tighter fit than the other lid types.

Since the specific object of this lid is to enclose the jar, measurements are of the utmost importance. The potter has to consider not only the angle or line of the neck and the shoulder, but also the *height* of the neck.

The throwing process for this lid is simple, but it takes careful workmanship to throw to specifications to make this lid fit properly. Skill in this matter is just as important—and as satisfying—as any other aspect of throwing. The beginning potter will have to try this lid a number of times to get a good fit both functionally and aesthetically.

TEAPOTS

MAKING A TEAPOT is the "big test" of a student potter's throwing experience and ability. The shape is considered by many to be the most difficult because it is made up of several parts which must fit together as a harmonious whole. Only repeated experiences, both in throwing and coordinating the separate parts, will produce satisfactory and pleasing results.

In addition to being attractive a teapot must function well. The strainer section must be capable of retaining the tea leaves, the lid must stay in place when the pot is tipped, and the handle must balance the pot. No wonder the teapot is a challenge! However, this shouldn't overwhelm the beginning potter. If he has conquerored the shapes dealt with previously, he already knows how to form the various parts which make up a teapot. The body and flanged lid were encountered in the lid section. The pulled handle and the lip on the spout were demonstrated in making a pitcher, and the spout itself is basically a part of the bottle shape, which also has been discussed. Making the strainer and applying the spout are the only technical aspects which are new, and these are not difficult to master.

Placement of the spout and handle—and this is very important—depends on the general shape of the pot and the relation of all the parts to each other. When planning placement, therefore, it always is best to have the lid in place since it, too, is part of the general effect. Here are three special points to watch in assembling a teapot:

1. Keep the bottom of the tip of the spout at the level of the rim or above it. If the spout level is lower than the filling level of the pot, tea will overflow from the spout.

2. Don't place the spout too low on the body. It may tend to become clogged with tea leaves.

3. A good-sized vent (a hole drilled or bored through the wall of the lid) acts as an air intake. If the lid fits very tightly, this is a necessity.

1.   The component parts for assembling a teapot are shown. The body and flanged lid are thrown first and, when leather hard, foot rimmed. The size and character of both the spout and handle are determined in relation to the body form with the lid in place.

2.   The spout is made exactly the same as the neck of a bottle; that is, it is constricted from the wide base to a smaller top. The pouring lip is pulled out while the clay is still soft. A small channel, cut to the center of the base, releases throwing water.

3.   When the spout is stiff enough to handle, it is cut diagonally from its base and held against the body to determine its position. The spout is trimmed to conform to the contour of the pot, and its placement on the pot marked with a pointed tool.

4.   The strainer is made by carefully boring holes well inside the areas marked for the spout. The holes are slanted down from the outside, to facilitate pouring, and made large enough to compensate for clay shrinkage and the addition of the glaze coating.

5.   If the wall of the pot is thick, excess clay is shaved from the strainer area with a thin-bladed knife. A thick wall area may affect the pouring quality of the teapot, producing a trickle instead of a stream of liquid from the pouring spout.

6.   The area where the spout is to be attached is dampened liberally with water, and the exact points of contact on both spout and pot are scored with the pointer to insure a good weld. These scored areas are coated with slip and the spout is attached to the pot.

7. A thin coil of clay is set around the spout and blended into the spout and the body. This not only assures a better weld between the two parts, but also gives the spout the appearance of growing out of the pot instead of having a "stuck-on" look.

9. The handle is detached from the supporting lump of clay and fastened to the pot. It, too, is blended into the body by adding small coils of clay at the points of contact. The assembled teapot and the lid are allowed to dry slowly in the damp box.

8. The handle is set directly opposite the spout, for visual as well as physical balance. A pencil is laid across the rim and the point of contact for the handle is marked on the pot. A damp cloth has covered this area up to this time to keep the wall from becoming too dry.

10. The teapot was bisque fired with the lid in place to avoid possible distortion, and then glazed and refired.

Courtesy, The Syracuse Museum of Fine Arts

TEAPOT by Robert H. Meinhardt

TEAPOT by Ruth Darrah

AN OVERHEAD HANDLE

AN OVERHEAD HANDLE is sometimes preferred for a teapot instead of the conventional pulled handle. While this handle *may* be made from clay, more often it is of another material— cane, reed, bamboo, metal or wire. Such a handle does not become a permanent part of the pot, but is attached to small clay loops or lugs that have been built onto the pot. A pre-shaped handle has adjustable, flexible wire ends for attaching to these lugs or coils.

Overhead handles can be made by the craftsman or they may be purchased ready-made from Oriental import stores or craft suppliers. They are so inexpensive and expertly made that most craftsmen prefer to purchase them.

Although the overhead handle is seen most often on the teapot shape, it also is used for covered jars and other specific shapes where a handle is necessary for function or is desirable for decorative purposes.

STONEWARE TEAPOT by John O'Leary

Courtesy, The League of New Hampshire Arts and Crafts

1. A pre-shaped bamboo handle is selected to fit the teapot in relation to both its character and size. The leather-hard pot is foot rimmed, the spout applied and the lid finished. A pencil-point mark indicates where the lugs are to be attached.

2. The areas on the shoulder where the lugs are to be placed are dampened with a sponge and the surface is scored or scratched with a pointer. Thick slip is added to the surface before the coils are attached to insure a strong, permanent weld.

3. The center of the coil is humped up, away from the body, to provide space for the ends of the handle to pass under. The ends of the coils are secured by pressing them down on the scored, slip-coated areas, using the round end of the modeling tool.

4. Finished teapot has a semi-matt white glaze. Overhead handles are used on other pottery shapes; cookie jars, ice buckets and flower containers are just a few shapes that might be enhanced by the use of the overhead handles made of clay or other materials.

Courtesy, The Henry Gallery, University of Washington

TEAPOT by John Polikowsky

TEAPOT by James Crumrine

LOW BOWLS AND PLATES

IN LEARNING to throw a low bowl or plate, the student encounters a difficulty not found in making a steep-walled bowl: as the wall is pulled *out* and thinned at a rather sharp angle, it may sag or collapse. This can be prevented by leaving a heavier wall thickness below the rim on the outside of the pot. This excess clay helps to support the shape while the piece is still soft. Later, when the foot rim is cut, this excess is tooled away. The inside of the bowl is given its *final* shape as the piece is thrown.

When the potter becomes more experienced and can work with assurance and rapidity, the amount of support clay left at the base can be lessened. Some potters throw these shallow forms by raising the wall into a rather deep bowl shape and then, in the final shaping, bringing it down to the desired low shape by pressure from the inside hand. Obviously, this method requires more practice and control, but it is a technique the student should try. The method presented here, however, is more practical for the less-experienced potter and should enable him to make these larger shapes successfully.

It is almost essential to throw the low bowl or plate on a large bat, since an attempt to lift it from the wheel head would result in distortion. And since extra clay is needed for support, the potter must start with a larger amount than is needed for the size of pot he has in mind. If the usual centering method seems awkward with a lump of this proportion, different methods should be tried to find one that is comfortable and effective.

Foot rimming may present new problems if the diameter of the leather-hard bowl exceeds that of the wheel head. In this case it is necessary to use an extension wheel head. This might be a large circle of masonite or plywood, or a large plaster bat. It is fastened to the wheel with thick slip.

If the wheel well is too small to accommodate the extension head, plaster bats can be stacked and fastened together with slip to "lift" the head out of the well.

When the slip hardens and the extension head is firmly fixed, concentric circles are marked on it with a pencil. These circles serve the same purpose as the concentric lines on the wheel head, to aid in centering the piece for foot rimming.

STONEWARE BOWL by Angelo C. Garzio

Courtesy, The St. Paul Gallery and School of Fine Arts

1. A large lump of clay is centered on a wide plaster bat attached to the wheel head. The lump is centered low and wide; the top hand is assisted by the wrist and part of the forearm in keeping the lump low and under control.

4. A roll of clay is brought up from the outside bottom to provide height and width. The amount brought up depends on how high and wide the bowl is to become. Enough clay must be left at the bottom to support the flaring shape.

2. Another method of opening is used for larger amounts of clay. The initial depression in the center is made by the thumbs, then the fingers of the right hand grasp the clay from the center and pull it back toward the potter.

5. The inside hand forces the clay wall outward to expand the diameter of the bowl. The left hand, starting at the center for each pull in order to maintain a continuous curve, increases its pressure for increased width.

3. The clay is pulled out, the shape sloping up toward the rim gradually, until the desired inside diameter is reached. Several pulls from the center may be necessary to complete the inside bottom.

6. The area immediately below the rim is thinned to the finished wall thickness, and the bowl is given its final shape. The bat and pot are removed from the wheel head and set aside to stiffen to the leather-hard stage.

7. The extension wheel head is used when the diameter of the bowl exceeds that of the wheel head. The leather-hard pot is measured, inverted, centered and fastened to the improvised wheel head.

8. The foot rim is cut and the outside surface finished with a sponge to soften or erase the footing marks. If the walls are uneven, after removing the bowl, the pot should be returned and trimmed some more.

STONEWARE BOWL by J. T. Abernathy

Courtesy, The Detroit Institute of Arts

Courtesy, The Wichita Art Association

STONEWARE BOWL by Raul A. Coronel

Courtesy, The M. H. DeYoung Memorial Museum

DECORATED FLAT BOWL by Raul A. Coronel

CLOSED FORMS

IF THE STUDENT is attracted by the small-necked bottle shape, he may discover even more adventure in working with *completely closed* forms. The object in making these is not to "use" the closed shapes as they are made; they serve merely as intermediate steps. By experimenting in shaping and cutting these forms, the potter may find that these so-called "useless" shapes can be *more* utilitarian than bottles. Some of the resultant forms that can be made from closed shapes are covered jars, salt and pepper shakers and hanging shapes such as planters and bird houses. Many more ideas will develop as the potter experiments.

The closed shape is an excellent exercise and a real challenge for both beginning and advanced students of the wheel. In addition to the technical skill developed from working with these forms, closed shapes test and promote the potter's creative ingenuity.

Salt and pepper shakers are made from small closed forms. Holes are drilled in the top for shaker openings, and a large hole is cut at the bottom for filling and for housing the cork that closes the base.

STONEWARE MASK POT by Toshiko Takaezu

Courtesy, The Cleveland Museum of Art

1. The top is formed as for a bottle shape, with a small length of neck rising above the shoulder. It is from this neck that the final closing of the shape is to be accomplished without causing the shoulder area to collapse or deform.

3. A fine sponge is used to help complete the closing. It rides the clay from the shoulder to the center, forcing just enough extra clay to the center to close it. Any slight modification in shaping can be done at this time.

2. The ends of the fingers constrict the clay of the neck to narrow the opening. If it is apparent at this stage that there isn't enough clay to close the form, the neck must be opened and the process started over again.

4. Before setting the pot aside to become leather hard, a small hole is made in the pot with a pointer. This provides some air circulation inside the pot and forestalls any possibility of a wall blowout as the clay shrinks.

5. Covered jar is a completely closed form with a small neck maintained and closed in. A small air hole is made at the point where the lid will be cut later. After the pot is leather hard, it is recentered on the wheel and fastened.

Covered jar results from a closed shape with a solid knob. When the top section of the form is cut out, a "self-covered" jar results. A flange is added to the lid for a better fit between jar and lid.

6. The lid is cut from the pot <u>on a slant</u>, using a pointer or sharp knife. The slant provides a seat or resting place for the lid. A small flange can be added inside the lid to provide a more secure fit.

Hanging planter is made by carving away portions of a closed form. The openings are large enough to permit easy planting and watering, but an enclosed area large enough to hold soil is left at the bottom.

CUPS AND SAUCERS

MAKING A SET of cups and saucers on the wheel involves principles of throwing already discussed. It also presents a new problem—that of fitting one form to another both physically and aesthetically.

The cup is a bowl or cylinder form with an attached handle, and the saucer is basically a low bowl or plate shape with a depression or inset in its center for holding the cup. These are simple things to make in themselves. However, the two forms must be related to one another. The cup must set in the saucer inset without wobbling, the handle must be placed for easy gripping and good balance, and the rim of the cup must be flared enough to make it easy to drink from.

The cups are thrown first. If they are to complete a set which includes a tea or coffee pot, their shape and style are determined to some extent by their relation to the parent form. To function properly, a cup must be easy to drink from. Consequently, this excludes a shape with a turned-in rim. On the other hand, a shape that flares widely at the top—while it may have an elegant appearance—allows a hot liquid to cool too rapidly.

The thickness of the wall must relate to the character of the design. A delicate shape would be contradicted by a heavy wall more appropriate to a sturdy mug shape.

The saucer must be wide enough to extend beyond the width of the cup to provide good balance—both visual and physical. The saucer rim must be high enough so that it may be easily gripped for lifting without having to be tilted. It should be deep enough to securely lodge a spoon beside the cup, but it should not be so high that the cup is hidden by the saucer. Finally, the saucer bottom must be thrown thick enough to allow for the tooled inset as well as the foot rim.

1. A cardboard measurement gauge is made of the width of the first cup foot rimmed and the rest of the cups in the set are footed to that size. Next, the saucers are recentered and fastened to the wheel.

2. The measurement cardboard of the cup foot rim is used for tooling the saucer insets. The inset diameter should be slightly larger than that of the cup foot rim to allow for easy cup placement.

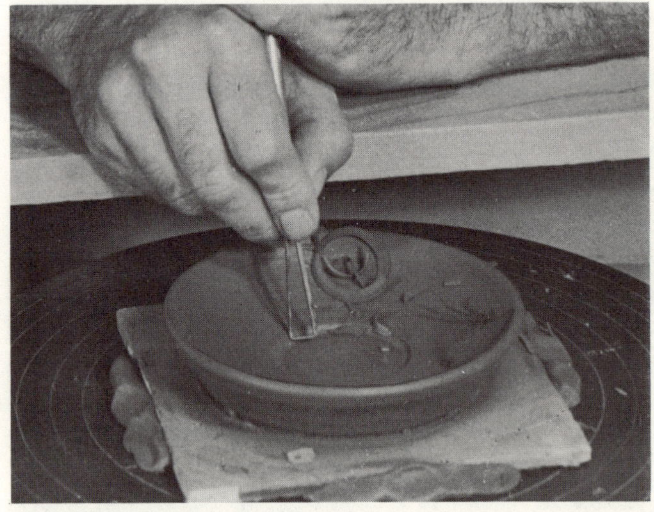

3. The inset is cut with the square-end tool. The inset should be deep enough to hold the cup firmly in place—about 1/8 inch. The bottom area must be level if the cup is to be well-seated.

4. A foot-rimmed cup is placed in the inset before the first saucer is removed from the wheel to make sure that the inset is functioning as desired. Then the rest of the saucers are tooled to match this measure.

6. The handles are attached to the cups to complete the set. The size of the handle must relate to the cup both in width and thickness; its placement must balance the cup and afford a secure grip.

5. The saucers are measured for thickness, then inverted on the wheel and foot rimmed. The foot rim should be slightly wider than the inset. A measurement is taken of the width of this foot and the rest are made to match.

Courtesy, The University of Illinois

STONEWARE TEA SET by Jim and Nan McKinnell

SECTIONAL POTS

IF A POTTER'S present skills do not permit him to make as tall a pot as he wants, he may try making such a pot from several sections. This is done by throwing two or more pots of a size suitable to his ability and, when they are leather-hard, welding these together vertically to form one tall pot.

Although this method is not difficult, there are two steps in the process that must be carefully observed. The first concerns the matter of *measurements*. The diameters of the rims to be joined together must be as near equal as possible if the sections are to be accurately joined. The second (and most difficult) concern is that of *contour*. The shape of the bottom section must be carried on and completed by any subsequent sections. Consequently, the thrown shapes must have a contour relationship if the finished pot is to have a unified shape. Both of these problems can be solved by careful planning and practice.

To make a sectional pot, the bottom section is thrown first. The diameter of the rim of this first section is measured with calipers; this measurement is for use in making the second section.

The first section is removed from the wheel and another cylinder is thrown for the second or top section. The width of this second cylinder near the base, where it is to join to the first section, must match the caliper measurement that has already been taken. Its shape also must correspond to the upper half of the planned form. After these are thrown, both sections are set aside until they reach an *early* stage of leather hardness.

PATIO SCREEN POSTS by F. Carlton Ball

1. Two leather-hard pots are ready to be assembled into a single tall pot. The top of the bottom section is measured with calipers, and this same measurement is located toward the base of the top cylinder, which is recentered on the wheel. The top section is cut from its base at this point.

2. The bottom section is returned to the wheel, centered and fastened with clay keys. Its rim is scored and covered with thick slip for joining to the top part. The bottom rim of the top section also is scored and brushed with slip before being set in place.

3. The top section is carefully set in place on the rim of the bottom section and gently rotated to make a firm joining. The wheel is rotated slowly so that the potter may check on the accuracy of the centering of the two joined sections.

4. A coil of clay is worked into the joining line to conceal the seam where the parts attach. After allowing the fresh added clay to stiffen for an hour or two, the excess clay at the seam is removed by tooling, and slight changes in the contour can be made.

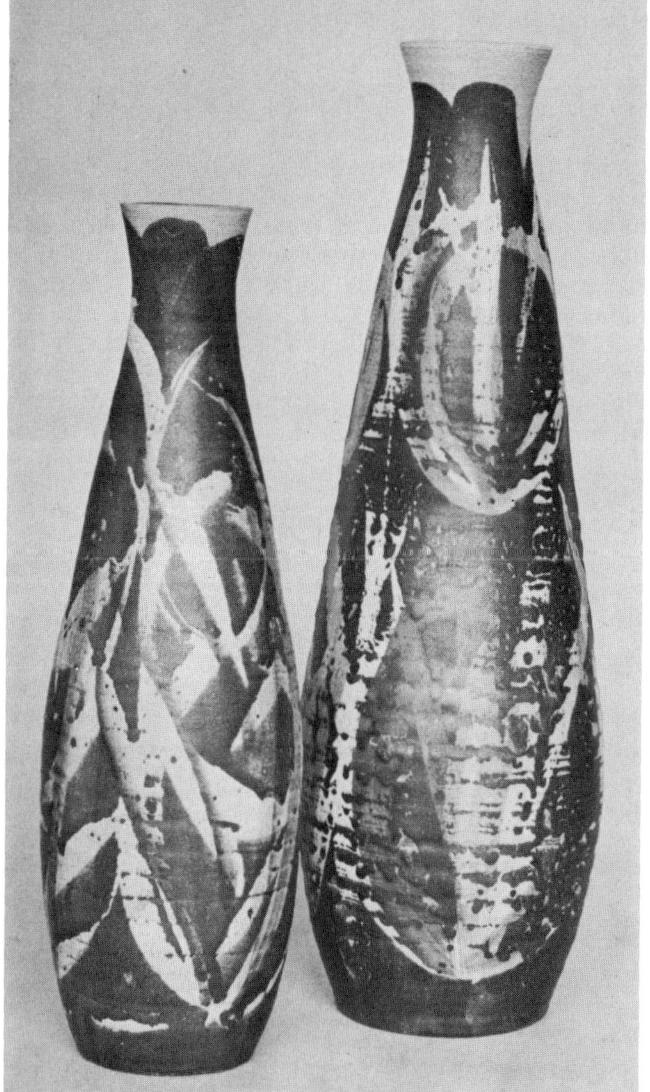

LUGGED BOWLS

A HANDLE that is quite different in form and appearance from the pulled handle is one that is thrown on the wheel and attached to the pot. The pulled handle functions best when placed opposite the spout; the thrown handle usually is placed at a right angle to the spout. The thrown handle is a useful one for such shapes as the teapot, pouring bowl, and cream pitcher. This thrown side handle is more serviceable and comfortable to use on small and medium-size pieces than on larger pots.

A side handle is thrown and applied to its pot in much the same manner as a spout is made and attached to a teapot. The potter must decide whether the pot is to be made for right or left-hand use. The left-hand handle is more comfortable for a right-handed person's use on forms like the pouring bowl, since a spoon generally is used along with it.

Experimentation is necessary to determine the proper placement of the handle on any given form. Some shapes require handles to be attached at particular levels either for appearance or comfortable balance. Usually, however, the handle will balance the pot best when it is placed at the halfway point of the pot, or slightly above it.

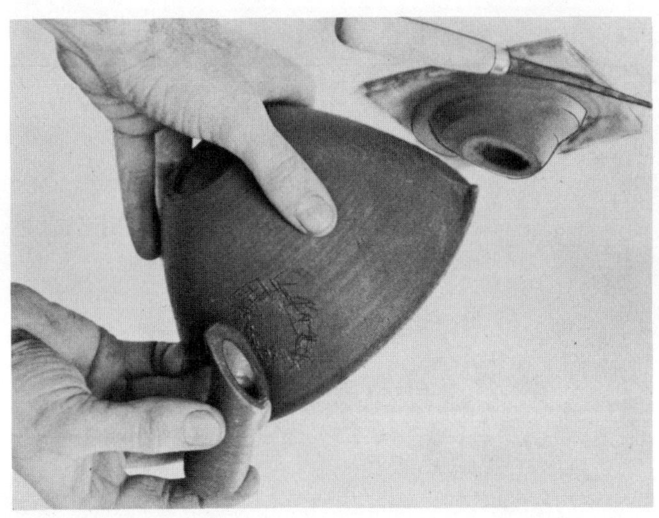

2. The handle is cut from its base at an angle and fit to the wall of the pot where it is to attach. It should be angled up slightly from the pot, and its placement should be placed at a right angle (or slightly forward) to the pouring lip. The pot and handle are scored and attached with thick slip where they meet.

3. After the handle is attached, the finished pot is returned to the damp box for slow drying. As a precaution against the weight of the handle causing it to crack away from the pot during drying, a stout clay coil or stilt is propped under the handle for support until the piece is almost completely dry.

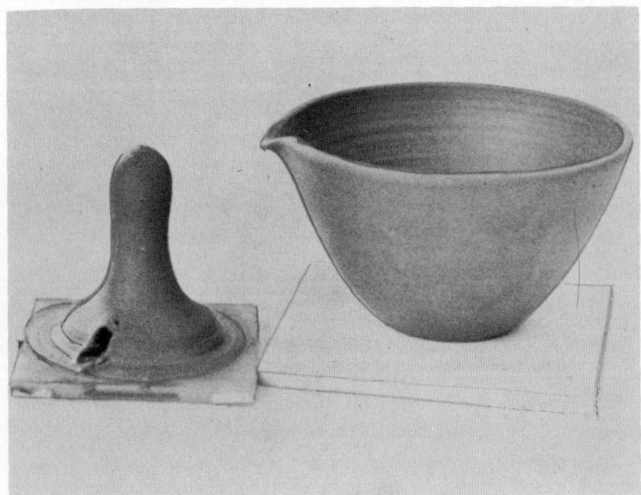

1. A bowl is thrown and a pouring lip is pulled at the rim (the same as for a pitcher). When it is leather hard, it is foot rimmed. The handle is thrown the same as for the teapot spout. A small channel made at its base allows the water to drain out and hastens the drying of the handle to the leather-hard stage.

DOUBLE-WALL POTS

ONE OF THE SPECIAL types of pots that beginners like to make is the flower pot with an attached saucer. Aside from a special appeal to plant enthusiasts, this flower pot project offers a unique throwing experience since it involves raising two walls from one lump of clay.

After a lump of clay is centered, the central portion is used to raise a flower pot section, and the small amount of clay left at the bottom is made into the attached saucer. When the piece is leather hard, the bottom of the saucer is foot rimmed and a small hole is drilled to connect the inside of the pot to the saucer. With the pot in actual use, this hole allows excess water to drain from the soil and into the saucer.

1. After the lump of clay is centered, a small amount of clay is left at the bottom while the larger upper portion is recentered into a lump of smaller diameter.

3. The saucer is made from the unused clay. A ridge is made by the finger just outside the wall of the pot, and the saucer wall is raised from this clay on the outside.

2. The outside bottom portion is left undisturbed; the upper section is opened and the wall is raised in the usual manner into a flaring cylindrical shape.

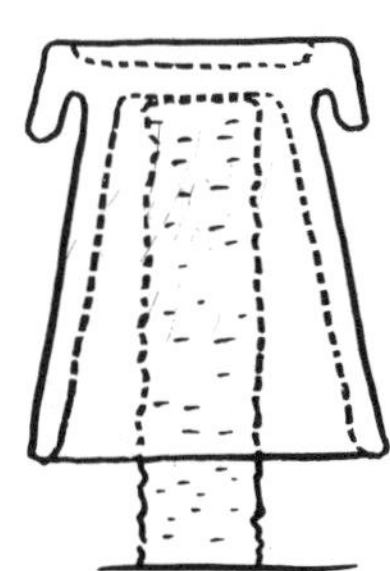

4. When the pot has been foot rimmed, a drainage hole is made (at an angle downward from the inside) to connect the base of the flower pot to the saucer.

5. If the inside of the flower pot is unglazed, the pot may be stilted upside-down in firing. This permits glazing of the bottom of the saucer.

MATCHED SETS

IN THROWING repeats of a shape, control of the clay and an accurate eye are the prime requisites. But the potter has two additional aids to help him achieve a reasonable uniformity in his pieces.

First of all, he can prepare in advance all the lumps of clay to be used. He makes sure that all the lumps are approximately the same size by judging them by sight or weighing each one on a scale.

Then, after he has thrown the first piece in a set, he can use a stick and calipers to measure the height and width of each piece as it is made. Measurements also are used to insure uniform foot treatment when the pieces are trimmed.

For the potter's first attempts to make matched sets, it is better to work with simpler shapes like the bowl, cup or tumbler. These are less difficult to duplicate than more-complex forms.

A certain amount of variation is inevitable when duplicates are thrown. No two pieces in a set will be identical—but then we don't particularly want them to be. Slight variations mark the thrown set as "handmade," contrasting to the uniformity of cast or jiggered ware.

Matched sets frequently introduce the potter to another design problem—relating the matched pieces to a different piece in a set. This may be a pitcher to accompany a set of tumblers, a teapot with a set of cups and saucers, or a jug to use with small juice or wine cups. The relationships in design among the components in such a set must be apparent, in order for them to belong together.

Glaze and decorative treatment help relate the various members of a set, but the basic concept of shape treatment is the primary consideration.

1. Four lumps of clay of equal size are weighed out in advance of throwing. While one lump is being thrown, the others are kept covered so they won't dry out.

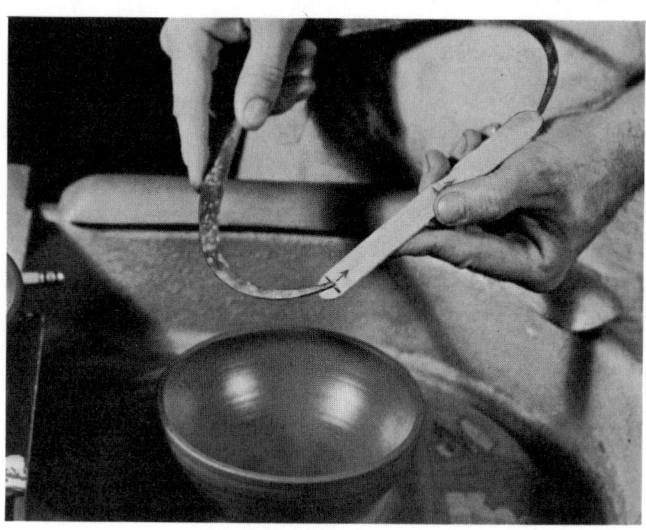

4. The width also may be set on the calipers, if the potter prefers to use this with or instead of the stick for measuring the width of his set of bowls.

2. After the first bowl is thrown, its measurements are taken. The height is marked off in pencil on a stick held vertically beside the thrown pot.

5. The second bowl is thrown with the first bowl nearby, so the potter can check on shape and wall thickness. The height measurement is referred to during the throwing.

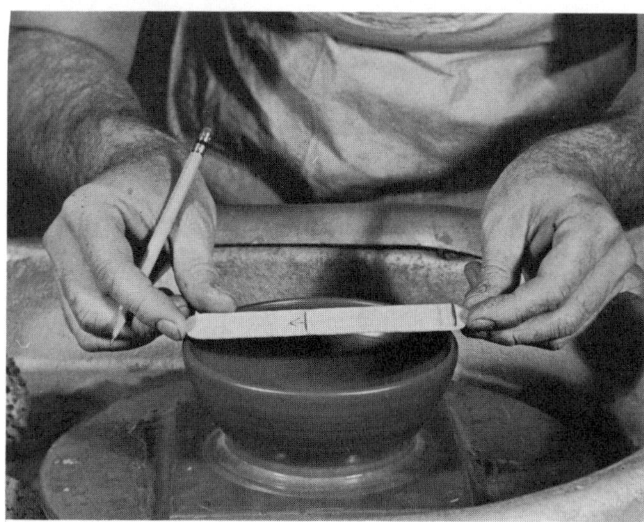

3. The width of the bowl at the rim is measured on that same stick. It is convenient to have both measurements together during the subsequent measuring procedures.

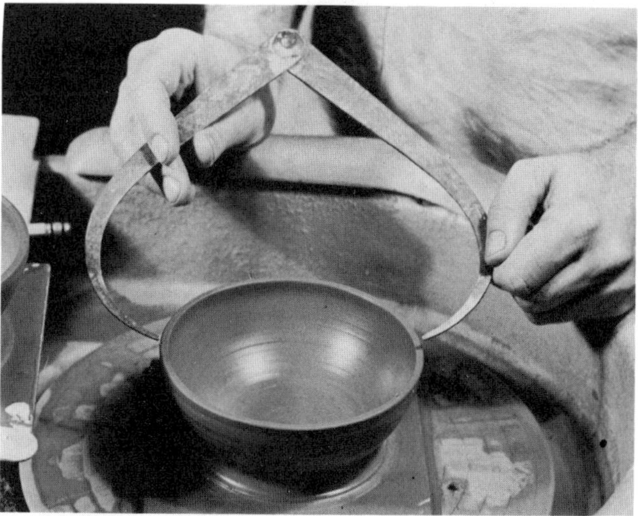

6. Width of the second bowl is checked against the caliper measurement of the first bowl. The rest of the bowls in the set are thrown and measured in this manner.

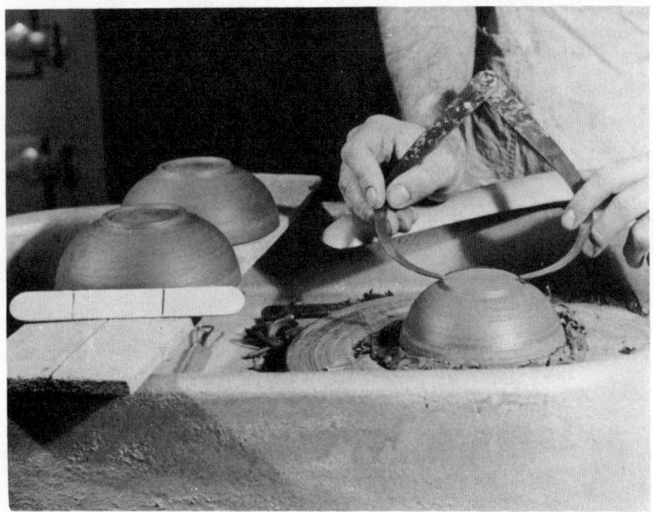

7. Bowls are foot rimmed when leather-hard. The foot is designed on one pot, and measurements of its height and width are taken on stick or calipers to use on the others.

8. Glaze treatment also helps relate the bowls in this set. The bowl interiors are glazed in a light green semi-gloss; the outsides are a soft green matt.

STONEWARE TEA SET by Toshiko Takaezu

Courtesy, The Detroit Institute of Arts

Courtesy, The Syracuse Museum of Fine Arts

STONEWARE JAR by Franz Wildenhain

Courtesy, Scripps College

BOTTLE by Dean Strawn   Courtesy, The Syracuse Museum of Fine Arts

EARTHENWARE BOWL by Edwin Scheier

Courtesy, The Syracuse Museum of Fine Arts

MELON SHAPED JAR WITH LID by Peter Voulkos   Courtesy, The M. H. DeYoung Memorial Museum

BOWL by Antonio Prieto

Courtesy, The Wichita Art Association

TWO-SPOUTED BOTTLE by Toshiko Takaezu

Courtesy, The St. Paul Gallery and School of Fine Arts

THOMAS SELLERS started writing a series of articles on the use of the potter's wheel in 1954 for publication in CERAMICS MONTHLY magazine. It is from these articles that the present handbook evolved.

Mr. Sellers is a native of Fort Wayne, Indiana. He received his M. A. degree in Ceramic Art from The Ohio State University in 1952. Since that time he has been director and pottery instructor at the City of Columbus Recreation Department's Arts and Crafts Center. He has participated in area and national ceramic shows, has had several one-man exhibitions, and has maintained a busy schedule of lectures and demonstrations on ceramics.

In September, 1960, Thomas Sellers was appointed editor of CERAMICS MONTHLY magazine; for several years previously he had served on the magazine's editorial staff.